Just Before Dawn

Hope for those who walk through the nighttime of abuse and its devastating aftermath

By

Pamela Perez

This book is a work of non-fiction. Names and places have been changed to protect the privacy of all individuals. The events and situations are true.

© 2003 by Pamela Perez. All rights reserved.

No part of this book may be reproduced, stored in a retrieval system, or transmitted by any means, electronic, mechanical, photocopying, recording, or otherwise, without written permission from the author.

ISBN: 1-4140-0513-X (e-book)
ISBN: 1-4140-0512-1 (Paperback)

This book is printed on acid free paper.

1stBooks – rev. 12/15/03

<u>Dedication</u>

This book is dedicated to

all those who help us make it through

And to those who would

if only they knew how

Acknowledgments

A special thanks to Alexandra Lindstrom, for all your hard work editing the manuscript, your input was invaluable. Thank you for your insights, and for your labor of love.

A special thank you also to Stephanie Wheeler, for the awesome work on the book cover. I am so proud of you!

To my family, thank you for your help, your encouragement, your input, and your tremendous courage in coming alongside me through the process.

Thank you, too, to all those who courageously and unselfishly shared their stories in this book. I could not have done this work alone.

Lastly, but certainly not least, I would like to thank the readers of this book. Our prayer for each of you is that this work here will enrich, encourage and equip you in every way.

Contents

Through the Silence 1
    If we would but stop and listen, what would we hear?
    Breaking the Silence

Questions 9
    Answers only come as a result of asking them
    Some questions we've asked...God, ourselves, others

Because 23
    If only we could explian it!
    Why God is trustworthy
    The effects of shame

Letters 43
    A Letter to my family
    A letter to my grandfather
    A letter to my counselor
    A Letter to my doctor
    A letter to my dentist
    A Letter to God
    A letter to myself

Kicking the Walls 61
The Walls of Secrecy
Walls of Denial
The Walls of Self-Protection
Walls of Frustration
Walls of Self-Determination
Walls of Self-Contempt
Walls of Despair
Walls of Fear
Walls of Anger/Rage
The Walls of Shame

Walls of Unforgiveness
Rebuilding the Walls

The Process 119
    What is the healing process?
  Coping and Coping Mechanisms
    Dissociative Identity Disorder (MPD)
    The way to hope
    Balm for the Hopeless
  More on Hope and Perseverance
  Out of the Depths
  Just Before Dawn

Helps 163
  From where does our help come?
  Some practical tools: Becoming informed
  Dissociative Disorders (DID)
  Post Traumatic Stress Disorder (PTSD)
  Dealing with depression
  Exercising our ability to choose
  Employing the appropriate use of the word *"No"*
  Setting healthy boundaries
  Learning to play
  The spiritual aspect of healing
  Guarding against Inner Lies
  Breaking unhealthy bonds and ties
  Seeking help for addictive behaviors
  Resisting isolation
  Establishing healthy relationships
  Taking care of ourselves
  Learning to accept help and fighting denial
  Knowing and accepting our limitations
  My part in the Body of Christ
  A word to therapists, support people, family members
  (and others who have been drafted into the process!)

The Battle 213
   The provision for victory
   Knowing your real enemy
   Ritual Abuse
   The Problem With Christian Symbols in SRA
   Once upon a time

Afterwards 232
   When comes the dawn at last

Foreword

Just Before Dawn fills a gap that has remained vacant for too long. It's a book about hope. There's always hope, even in the Valley of the Shadow. . . because "God is with me." Thank you, Pamela, for sharing your heart & for being so candid and compelling about what you have learned. God's light emanates from this book, and in His light we can stay on His pathway.

As a therapist, I have met people who have suffered greatly. Some of them have been challenged and encouraged by the message of this book. The book "made me cry, it gave me words for the questions I could not ask, and it told my story as it needed to be told." My fellow therapists have given me nothing other than enthusiastic approval. One of them put it this way, "It is a book that is worth reading. Every part of it is important for therapists."

I expect that very soon our culture will no longer be able to avoid facing the suffering that so many of us have been through. When that day comes it will not about finding the right therapist. We don't need more therapists; we need people who can spread God's grace in the midst of a suffering world. This book brings hope because it spreads God's grace. Upon reading *Just Before Dawn,* you will be a little closer to God, and, as was the case for Moses, God's light will reflect from your countenance. That is where God's grace has its source. Pamela is such a person and so is this book. If you read it expect to glow!

James G. Friesen, PhD

Just Before Dawn

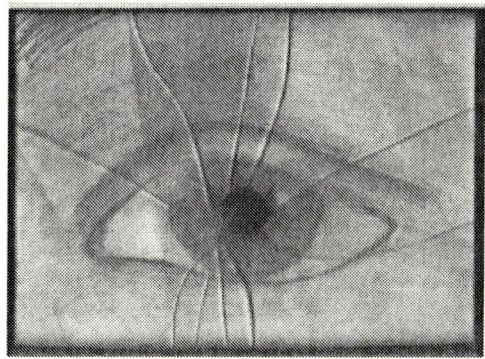

By Jen

Through the Silence

*Through the silence,
if one would but stop
and listen,
a voice, distant and small...
Its tenor is plaintive and hesitant,
fearing detection or even acknowledgment,
and yet praying for it all at the same time.*

*Through the silence,
God is speaking, as well.
Longing, yearning to be heard,
whispering softly and lovingly to His beloved ones,
drawing them to Himself.*

Every survivor of abuse knows about silence - the dead stillness in the house at night that wraps its cold arms around the silent soul of a child who is too afraid to cry out. The silence of family members who either know, or at least suspect that something isn't quite right, yet respond with nothing but more silence.

Silence is often the protective device of choice for those who have learned that breaking silence can be a dangerous thing; yet, unless we

Through the Silence

break the long silence, the secrets remain intact and will continue to keep us bound up and far from healing.

One survivor wrote about it this way:

> *It was in the darkest part of my lifetime, the place where silence was loudest, that I knew the time had come to break the long silence at last. What I eventually had to come to terms with was that I had believed the lie that if I broke my silence, it would surely result in my complete annihilation and ruin. I had been bound by that belief long enough! Instead, I finally understood that my silence was breaking me.*
>
> *So I dared to speak. For the first time ever, I broke every rule I'd ever been taught by speaking my pain out loud, speaking my memories, and telling someone about the horrors of my past. It was an extremely difficult thing to do. I took the chance, though. Because I did, I found my voice again and I was able for the first time in my life to hear other voices than the cruel ones inside me. For the first time, I heard hope. And as a result, I healed.*

If breaking the silence is indeed the way to healing, what keeps the walls of silence so intact? What is it that we have come to believe about ourselves that leaves us bound and gagged in self imposed prisons of mute despair? This is something we must be willing to consider carefully if we are to break free from the fetters that hinder the freedom God intended for us to have all along. We must ask ourselves then, audibly, the questions that demand an answer.

What keeps me so far away, at times even willing myself not to hear?

If I should dare to stop and listen, what then?

Why am I so afraid?

*Is it shame? I don't want to feel that way again, ever!
The terrible sting of the humiliations they forced upon me...
And what if I tell...and you shame me, too?*

*Will you tell me I am beyond repair? Too far gone, spoiled,
damaged goods,
disqualified by my past?*

What if you speak kindly to me? I'm afraid of that, too - perhaps even more!

What if I get my hopes up? What if I begin to believe, begin to hope, begin to rise from my dark place, and then, disappointment comes again, or my fears become realized?
What if I don't really know you at all? What if I think you will hear me if I speak, and then you refuse and walk away? What then?

*And what about God?
I mean, what if I've been mistaken about Him?
What if I heard wrong?
After all, I can't trust me, I know that...*

*All that's left is my fear
Of trusting when I shouldn't
Of believing the wrong thing
Of being deceived again
Of more pain...*

Maybe keeping the silence is best...

We will discuss some of these and other such questions in a section dedicated just for that purpose, but unless we are willing to take the first steps in breaking the silence we cannot hope to find the answers our hearts crave. So many of us have lamented, "How often I wish I could talk to someone, to express the depths of my heart's emotion, pain, frustration, hopes, dreams! But I'm afraid. Silence binds me, enfolds me like a shroud. There are no words to adequately express what I feel. Or if I should dare to speak, would anyone even listen

Through the Silence

without rejection, or anger, or judgment, or blame, or condemnation, or making me feel unjustly responsible for their reaction to my experiences, feelings, thoughts, responses to my abusive past?"

For too many of us, the cruel lessons about keeping silent have been reinforced again and again, not only by our abusers but also by well-meaning friends and family. Until telling our stories of struggles and abuse is acceptable, healing cannot occur within the context of relationships as God intends. We need to be free to share our hearts, weaknesses, fears and concerns somewhere other than the counselor's office. Healing must take place within healthy relationships, in fellowship with the rest of the body of Christ, so that we can heal in the midst of an atmosphere of unconditional love, acceptance and safety.

In *Living From The Heart Jesus Gave You*, Dr. James Friesen stresses this very concept. Growth, repair, maturity, and faith development are all intimately tied to relationships. People do need people to achieve wholeness in a fractured world" (6).

Yet we remain silent and hidden and trapped in our pain, "all alone in the crowd." All too often, we hide behind well-practiced smiles and a surface politeness because we believe that speaking aloud what we see inside of us would risk the condemnation, criticism, and rejection we so intensely fear.

What happens when we choose to remain silent, when we will not call out for the help we most certainly will need in order to become whole? Perhaps this next dialogue between God and *the little lamb* will help to describe that:

> Little lamb, little lamb,
> where did you go?
>> *To hide in the cleft of the Rock.*
>> *But on my way I slipped and fell*
>> *and now am not able to walk.*

Just Before Dawn

Little lamb, little lamb,
Why do you weep?
Why do you pine and mourn?
> *My despair is deep, my sadness great,*
> *all about I am wounded and torn.*

I cannot walk without a limp
or leaning on a staff,
I cannot help myself at all
and my enemies mock and laugh
They joy to see me in my plight
with all my sin revealed,
and glory in my near demise -
they think my fate is sealed!

Me, I'm not so very sure
the cruel end will come,
any yet, so much is now in doubt -
I have no place to run,
no place to hide from all my pain,
no one to hold it fast
and keep it from devouring me
as I recall my past.

If only I could lock it back
within the darkened cell!
If only sweet forgetfulness
would ease me from my hell
and cure the other pains and hurts
remembering has brought -
for I have lost the very things
that I have always sought.
I have not been the blessing that
I always longed to be,
Instead I've robbed and maimed and hurt
the ones most dear to me.

Through the Silence

> *Will God redeem such wretchedness?*
> *Forgive such foolish waste?*
> *Will God restore such utter loss?*
> *or simply turn away...*

The psalmist expressed it well when he wrote again and again of the intense pain that such silence brought.

"But when I was silent and still, not even saying anything good, my anguish increased. My heart grew hot within me, and as I meditated, the fire burned; then I spoke with my tongue" (Ps 39:2-3 NIV).

It cannot be done alone. Silence must be broken. All the pain and despair must find a safe outlet. The concept of joy, so foreign to so many of us, must be introduced within the loving context of the body of Christ.

> Little lamb, little lamb
> I see where you've been -
> But what will you do now?
> > *I fear to hope, I dare not trust,*
> > *to wish is not allowed...*
>
> Dear little lamb
> for whom I've come
> to save and to restore,
> New life I long to give to you
> and peace, and joy, and more!
> If only you would finally let
> Me ease you from your pain!
> Please let My people come beside,
> And show you Who I Am!

"To you I call, O LORD my Rock; do not turn a deaf ear to me. For if You remain silent, I will be like those who have gone down to the pit. Hear my cry for mercy. I call to you for help, as I lift up my hands toward your Most Holy Place" (Ps 28:1-3).

Breaking The Silence

*Perhaps it's time to break the silence -
For silence is breaking me...
If I dared, would it avail me?
Would I indeed be free?
Free to heal and to recover,
Free to finally seek
Some answers to the questions in me
I've never dared to speak?
Perhaps at last God will exchange
Those things I knew before
For higher truths and purer hopes
And nobler goals; restore
my wounded soul and broken heart
and devastated mind,
redeem my life from death's fast grip,
My inner sorrows bind.
If I should speak and break the rules
That silence keeps in place,
What would result? What would I find
Behind this plastic face?*

God has an answer for our desperate heart's cry:

"And call upon me in the day of trouble: I will deliver thee, and thou shalt glorify Me" (Ps 50:15 KJV).

Through the Silence

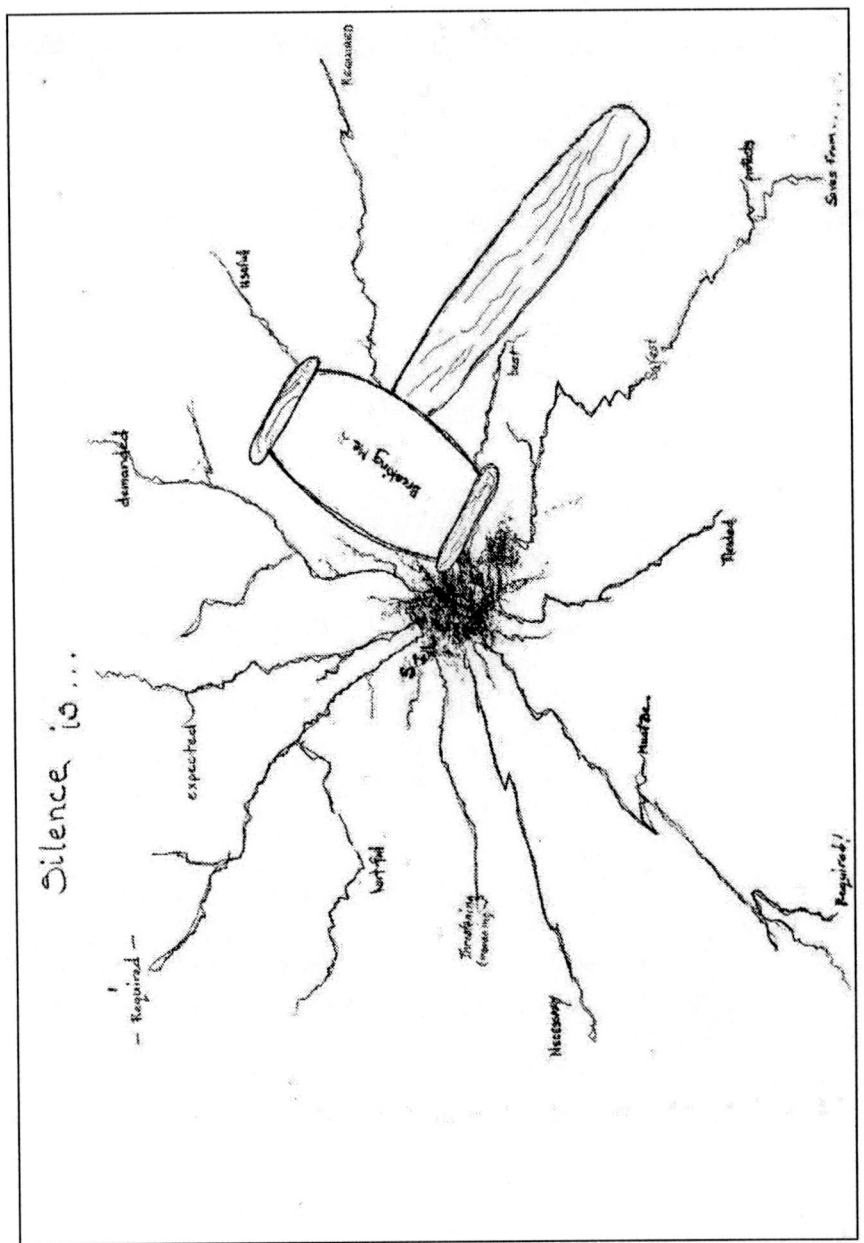

Silence is Breaking Me

Questions

"And now, Lord, what am I waiting for?" Psalm 39:7

"I never said to you, 'Seek Me in vain.'" Isaiah 45:19

"I remember the day I approached my mother and asked her how Jesus' dying on a cross almost two thousand years before could possibly cover my sins. She was horrified. She told me I was going to Hell. Believe me, I was very careful not to ask questions like that again! But worse, the most important question that anyone can ever ask didn't get answered. And since I was apparently condemned, it didn't seem to matter anymore anyway." Ann

Questions. Answers only come as a result of asking them.

The problem for many of us is that, all too often, we don't even know what the questions are! Or if we do, we're ashamed or afraid to ask them - at least out loud.

Our God *invites* us, over and over again throughout the scriptures, to come to Him with our questions, our concerns, our confusion, distress, fear, and to bring to Him our petitions. He places no qualifiers or constraints upon us, and turns no earnest seeker away, no matter what the nature of the inquiry. He understands our need to ask questions. He also understands our hesitancy to ask them.

Questions

I wish I had all the answers
For all that ever was,
I wish I possessed all the wisdom
To understand all that God does.

Questions

I wonder why He allowed it
To happen the way that it did?
Why didn't someone protect me?
Why doesn't God simply rid
My life of these painful memories
And all of the harm that was done?
Why do I feel so discouraged?
Why does it seem like 'they' won?
Why do they tell me God loves me
When it isn't something I feel?
Why can't I get better faster?
When will I finally heal?
What if I trust and it hurts me
The way many others have done?
What if I find I'm mistaken
And find there is nowhere to run?

If I should ask God my questions
What would He do to me?
What will the church people say then?
What kind of sin would that be?
Would I harshly be punished
For failing to trust what they say?
Would I be cut off forever
And once and for all sent away?

Some might ask, "How could anyone feel this way? We all have questions, don't we?" Most of us are absolutely spilling over with them! And yet, asking questions isn't always a safe thing to do, especially for those who have felt the sting of censure for asking them.

The problem, then, isn't having questions, but where and to whom we can ask them. If only more people understood that we know that there aren't always easy answers, sometimes we just need to be heard.

For others, we may have a gnawing sense of wanting answers, but we can't define the questions clearly enough to convey them. Unless we stop long enough to listen inside so that we can formulate the questions, however, we will be like those setting off on a journey without first knowing the destination. The answers, like the goal, will continue to evade us.

Some questions don't have an answer - at least not ones we can always grasp, here and now. Our finite nature limits us and limits our understanding, because we cannot possibly see the whole picture. That kind of knowledge is not available to us. Like Job, we can only see today, and what that feels like right now. "My life is over," he lamented in chapter 19. That was genuinely what he saw and felt at that time and place in his life. His life, in fact, was far from over, but who could have told him differently? His "friends" had no more ability to predict the future than he did. In fact, they were so far away from understanding the present situation that they certainly did more harm than good! It may be a good idea, then, to read *Safe People,* by Cloud and Townsend, (listed in Resources section) for some guidelines on how to choose to allow into our lives those people who can walk through our questions with us and not do us more harm by unintentionally trying to fix or explain it all when that simply cannot be done.

Below are some of the questions others have asked. Perhaps you've asked them, too. The important thing for each of us, individually, personally, is to get still enough for long enough to know what the cry of our hearts sounds like, to heed it, and then to set out on a bold quest in seeking the answers. And while we may not find the answer to every question, we must not let that stop us - there are so many answers we *can* find!

Some questions we've asked God

God, I have questions! Is that allowed?

I want to ask You – WHY?!?

Questions

Why me?
Why now?
Why them?

Why not?!
Why not give up?
Why not quit?

Why isn't it getting better faster?

Why don't more people get it?

Lord, do You want to help me?

Am I worth enough to be saved from this pit?

Why do You talk about the recovery process, the healing,
joy, and peace,
yet every second, every minute, wherever I go, wherever I turn
I am back where I started,
always feeling this awful ache in the center of my chest,
full of pain and hurt.
What is wrong with me?

Are You playing games with me, Lord?

Why did you make me this way? To be set up, put down, taken advantage of? I'm angry with You for making me!

What am I doing wrong? Your expectations seem so high. I am trying to do the right thing but I fail. Just tell me what I am doing wrong!

Why do You always show me Your back when I try to imagine You? I want to know You, but You keep turning from me. Why won't You show Yourself? You're supposed to help me.

Just Before Dawn

If You're God, then do something! Why are You so passive when it comes to defending me?

Will I ever feel loved and accepted by You, Lord?

I can't ever meet Your standards. Why do You make it so difficult to follow You?
I read about a compassionate, loving God, but I can't see that. Am I that blind?

Why is it so hard to believe Your word? It just doesn't sink in.
I just can't believe that You love me no matter what.
I believe in Your word, God. It's just that it is hard to believe or understand Your character.

I Just Can't Reach You

Questions

Fears

I'm afraid of You, God.
   I don't know what You'll ask next
      Or where You'll take me
         And perhaps leave me alone there...
I'm afraid You'll hurt me
   And then demand that I be strong
      And not complain
I wish I could curl up safely to Strength
   Without demands
   Or judgment
   Or condemnation
   Or shame
Maybe I don't really know You at all
Like Paul, I say, Who are You, Lord?

Dear reader, please ask! Ask God. The answers may not come right away, or as clearly or as easily as we would like. We may not find all the answers, but if we do not allow ourselves to honestly ask God the hard questions, we may not find any answers at all, and that would be a considerable loss. We need to settle the issue that, despite what abuse taught us, asking questions is allowed, and right, and acceptable, and good. Best of all we, have an all wise God Who is willing to be asked, and abundantly patient in doing so in a way that will bring us hope and health and a peace that passes understanding. It may be scary at first, but experiencing the loving response of a gentle Teacher, we will find our fears exchanged for a new confidence and joy in the One Who alone has all answers. Ask on!

Some questions we've asked ourselves

Who am I?
I look in the mirror and whom do I see?
It's someone I don't know, certainly not me.

Lots of people stare out at me.
Who am I?
One of us doesn't know Jesus and doesn't trust Him,
Another keeps praying,
and yet a couple more are singing in the background.
    Chaos and pandemonium seem to reign.
    I can't hear God, there is too much noise.
    Shut up!
    Listen, okay?
        Why am I like this? Why can't I just change?
        People try to tell me the "right" thing to do, but I don't do it. I can't. Why?
            WHY?!?

English 311 (Study of the English Language)
by Lexy

I feel strangely sane
although
I sit in linguistics class
and fight
a sudden urge to scream -
overpowering.
The propensity for language is
innate.
Or so I must say to earn an A.
If speech is inborn,
why can't I find my voice?
My mind is drowning
cesspools of guilt, shame, and pain
and the only words I've learned,
"Great! And how are you?"

Questions

Confusion
By Stela

Who am I Lord? Why am I here?
Is life to love, or something to fear?
What use am I, what good can I do?
Why am I living? When will I die?

A life of confusion, so utterly marred...
Though outwardly I hide my innermost scars.
Why am I like this? What made me this way?
Why do I fight life with every new day?

Why do I flee that which I seek?
Why am I scared of the hope that I speak?
Why do I fear love, laughter and joy
And view other's kindness as a threatening ploy?

Why do I feel so lost and alone?
When will I ever find my way home?

Some questions we've asked others

Why do you ask me what I need and then get mad for telling you?

Why do you tell me just to get over it when you've never done it yourself?

Why do you so quickly quote me a verse instead of just listening when you ask me what's wrong?

Why do you treat me as if I'm a second-class Christian, like I am an exception to the promises of God, or beyond hope and healing?

Why are you so quick to judge and assume when you have never walked where I must?

I want to know Jesus, to ask questions about God, to clear up the confusion in my head, but how can I if you rebuke and shame me for it?

While it is not our intention to glibly pass out quick answers to questions like these in this section (they don't exist anyway), we do hope that you will find answers to at least some of them, and comfort in knowing that you are not alone on this journey. Know what hinders you from asking, from daring to voice your questions and concerns, and then let God surprise you with His joy as He directs you to Himself in your quest. He promises that He will not shame, nor forsake, nor reject, nor will He turn away in frustration or disappointment. *"God is not a man that He should tell or act a lie, neither a son of man, that He should feel repentance or compunction (reluctance or unwillingness) for what He has promised. He has said, and shall He not do it? He has spoken, and shall He not make it good? (*Num 23:19 Amp) He shall! There is no greater joy to the Heavenly Father's heart than for His children to trust Him with their questions, cares, and concerns. Matthew 7:7-11 is a wonderful testimony to the faithfulness of our gracious God. He Himself is the One Who invites us to come.

"Ask, then, that ye might receive, and that your joy might be full!"
John 16:24

This next poem was written by a survivor to her counselor. What a priceless gift this dear woman gave the one in her care when she allowed her, without shaming or judgment or giving up, to reveal her true self by hearing her questions.

<u>To My Counselor</u>
By Linda

I have hid for so long.
Would you know me if you saw me?
Would I know myself?

Questions

> *It is scary as I try.*
> *Will you like me if you see me?*
> *Will I like myself?*
>
> *It's bumpy as I go.*
> *Will you wait while I learn?*
> *Will I be able to wait?*
>
> *I want to run and hide again.*
> *Will you help me stay and face it?*
> *Will I let you help me?*
>
> *I want to be free.*
> *Will you hold on to the hope for me?*
> *Will I dare to hope?*
> *It hurts so much to be out here.*
> *Will you go slow and not hurt me?*
> *Will I accept it?*
>
> *Some day there will be an end.*
> *Will you still be there with me?*
> *Will I believe it?*

What about outside of the counselor's office? Will we find those who will accept us even when we don't wear our *"OK Face"* the way others have come to expect? Who would want or accept someone who doesn't always "have it together" all the time? The fear of not being the "right" one can be absolutely terrifying for many of us.

__Who Would Want...__
by Lexy

I'm the smart one. The one with the answers and insight.
I'm the funny one. I keep my friends in stitches.
I'm the understanding one. A good listener - that's me.
I'm there through thick and thin; I don't let others down.
Now, I want to talk about me, the things of matter and meaning.

Pins shoved through my hands should I cry.
Endless days and nights locked in closets with roaches.
Kitten's blood trickling over my chest.
My last sight for months - bleach dripping into my eyes.
I want to talk about the things that made me into ME.
But who would want that?
I'll be the smart one, the funny one, the understanding one.
I'll be the one you want around.

This leads to another key question: What if I'm not (at least perceivably) "the one" you want around? What then? It is questions like these that we absolutely must face, though it can honestly be terrifying to do so. We must dare to ask them so that the answers are at long last found. It is important that we understand that it is normal for those who have been hurt in such ways to feel the isolation that "being different" seemingly locks us into. Believing we are worthless unless we measure up to the expectations of those who have hurt us for not doing so is a root in our belief system that runs deep and is not easily eradicated.

God asks questions, too

Adam, where are you? Why are you hiding?

It's a good question. Why *do* we hide? Especially from God. Who made us believe we had to?

From the very beginning, back there in the garden, Satan has spent the years since Adam and Eve doing his best to create distrust and separation between God and His people. The cruel suggestions whispered to Eve continue to be heard by us to this very day! "Are you *sure* God really has your best interests in mind? *Are* you sure He is not withholding something from you? *Did* God *really* say…"?

Unless we know the truth about God, Who He is, what He did and did not say, what His character is like, we will not be able to withstand the lying insinuations of the enemy against Him to us!

Questions

Jesus asked questions of those He came in contact with, followers and critics alike - some very pointed ones at times!

"Whom do the people say that I am?"
Now here's an interesting consideration. Things were becoming more and more stirred up around the whole issue of the identity and status of Jesus of Nazareth. He recognized that this would certainly affect His disciples, and He confronted the issue head on. People most certainly will see things from their own viewpoint and perspective and beliefs. It will affect us, one way or another. This is simply human nature and to be expected. But the next question Jesus asks Peter is the bottom line for each of us individually.

"Whom do YOU say that I am?"
Whom do we say Jesus is? It's not so hard to believe He's the Messiah up on the mountainside while He miraculously feeds massive crowds with minuscule provisions, but what about afterwards, when the miracle hour has passed and we're back down trying to find sustenance in the scraps available to us as the result of our own exhausting labor?

When sickness strikes, then Whom do we say Jesus is?

When friends and family misunderstand and unfairly criticize us, then Whom do we say that He is?

When we are exhausted from lack of sleep due to nightmares and insomnia, when our abusers deny any wrongdoing, when our whole world seems to have been turned upside down because of horrible memories and flashbacks and crushing depression and discouragement and inner turmoil and pain, *now* Whom will *I* say that Jesus is *to me personally?*

For each of us, it will come down to how we answer this question, for ourselves, one on one with God, in the very deepest part of us where only He can go.

Often it is the very crisis of our healing process that will force us into the place of resolution of this issue once and for all, and that is a good thing (even if it feels quite awful).

God invites us over and over again to ask Him the hard questions, to share with Him the issues upon our hearts and in our lives, to wrestle through to completion anything that might keep us from coming to terms with Who He is - and who we are in light of that truth. So much hinges on it, let us not miss out on what He wants to gift us with as a result of seeing the struggle through!

"Ask of Me...Seek Me...Pray..." (Ps. 2:8, Isa. 45:11, Matt. 7:7 and 8, Jn. 14:14, etc.)

"This is the confidence we have in approaching God; that if we ask anything according to His will He hears us." I Jn. 5:14

"If any one lacks wisdom, let him ask it of God, Who gives to all liberally, without finding fault." Jms. 1:5

We *should* ask our questions! If we allow ourselves to be that honest, answers will come.

Nativity
By Leigh

At the bottom of the pit
In the blind
malignant dark
conceived of grief
and wretched desperation
is born a babe
whose cry is weak
but sure...

Her name is Hope

Questions

I'm holding onto a smooth, round ball. Gripping it. Hard. So no one can take it away from me. It's *mine*. But then suddenly my ball is not the same anymore. It hurts. Sharp, steel spikes are piercing my skin. I want to drop it or throw it onto the ground only- I can't. It's mine. Scarlet drops fall slowly to the dirty floor. It hurts so bad that I think I'm going to be sick. Doesn't anyone see that I'm bleeding? Doesn't anyone care. I know it's mine. But won't someone help me? Please? Please.

By Beth

<u>Because</u>

***"Because Thy loving kindness is better than life
my lips shall praise Thee" (Ps. 63:3).***

What a wonderful verse. What a wonderful conclusion to be able to come to.

But what about those who cannot, who have not yet gotten to this place? What if we still struggle with issues about God, about life, about love, about the point of any of it?

And what about those outside would-be support people who wish to come alongside the wounded and help them with such issues? How do we go about helping *them* understand why we feel as we do, why we struggle with the things we do, and why we react the way we do?

"If only I could explain it!" we often lament. "If only I could make someone understand!" The problem is, trying to put into words what for most trauma survivors is beyond description is no small task!

In this section we'd like to address the age-old question, *"WHY?"* Not because we believe we have all the answers, we do not; we certainly can address at least some of them. Hopefully, understanding will bridge the gap between us.

When one survivor was asked why she felt she didn't have the freedom to share her questions and struggles with others, she wrote about it this way:

> *They just don't get it.*
> *How can I describe what it's like inside me?*
> *If they knew they would...*
> *What?*
> *Because of what I've experienced already,*
> *I'm afraid to even think about it!*
> *How do I know, you ask?*
> *Because I've lived it, I've experienced it -*

Because

> *the rejection, the silence, the looking away, the quick change of the subject...*
> *People don't know what to do with my pain, or how to respond to issues of abuse.*
> *They're uncomfortable.*
> *I don't blame them.*
> *But it still hurts.*

In this section we'd like to share just a few of the *"becauses"* that may help those who have not experienced abuse understand our "necessary" way of doing life. To a survivor, they make perfect sense (once we get to the core of the issue). Perhaps they will to you, the reader, as well.

G.S., another abuse survivor, writes this:

> Because I was in the state of mind and body you describe here, I know that I was pressed into finding ways to seek healing.
> I knew that God was saying, "Enough!" He chose to separate me from my abusive marriage and send me to church with a good friend that took me there every Sunday. God then moved me to join a Christian church where I discovered and read a book by a woman who wrote about forgiveness. It helped my state of mind tremendously. After that, I read the New Testament several times and I prayed a lot. I was then able to talk more to people. I was brought out of myself by God Himself. He then led me to help others.

> I do recall these feelings - some more than others, and some are still with me and always will be. I know for a fact that it takes a long time to heal the deep wounds, and then you have to learn to live with the scars. Since the time I started the healing process up to the present day I'm now able to say that "I'm almost normal." According to my family, I do things weird or different sometimes that boggles their minds, I know it's hard for them to understand. It's because...

<u>Let me explain…</u>

Because I've been so wounded I'm afraid of more pain.
  I'm afraid to be seen as weak.
    I must be strong at all costs.

Because I've been betrayed I'm afraid of people.
  I'm afraid to need anyone.
    I must remain fiercely independent.

Because I've been lied to I'm afraid of being deceived.
  I don't even trust myself.
    I dare not depend on anyone or anything.

Because I've been hurt when somebody 'saw' me I'm afraid to be seen.
  I'm afraid to make noise.
    I must never call attention to myself.

Because I've been punished for being weak I'm afraid to ask for help.
  I'm afraid to be alone but I have to be.
    I cannot allow myself to need anyone.

Because I've been blamed I tend to feel overly responsible for everything that happens around me.
  I'm afraid of making mistakes.
    It's my own fault anyway.

Because I've been punished for doing or feeling what someone didn't allow I'm indecisive
  I'm afraid to choose.
    I must never make a decision somebody might not like.

Because I've been humiliated again and again I feel deeply, inherently ashamed.
  I'm afraid of making eye contact.
    I dare not remove my mask of pretense.

Because

Because others lost control and hurt happened as a result of it I must never get angry or lose my temper.
  I'm afraid to make people mad at me or to disappoint them or feel their disapproval.
    I must watch, listen, be on guard every minute.

Because going to bed at night was not safe I am afraid to go to sleep.
  I'm extremely hyper-vigilant, I startle so easily.
    I must watch every move, constantly look out at every direction.

Because I feel so powerless I am easily depressed.
  I'm afraid of not being in control.
    I must be submissive and not fight back, it only makes things worse if you do.

Because carrying such a heavy load is too much to bear, I'm weary and exhausted.
  I'm afraid of being considered lazy.
    I must never be too easy on myself, I just don't deserve it.

Because life has had to be something I took very seriously I have a hard time playing.
  I'm afraid to relax or let my guard down and be accused of being silly.
    I have no right to laugh or have fun.

Because there is such an intense war going on within me I am ambivalent.
  I'm not sure what I want sometimes, I can't decide what to do.
    I feel like the weight of responsibility I bear will crush me.

Dear reader, this is only a sample of what goes on in an abuse survivor's mind! Is it any wonder that the basic issues like trust and interdependence are so difficult to attain? For those who have experienced such betrayal and who have been denied having the basic human needs of love and acceptance and safety met, these are extremely difficult obstacles to overcome.

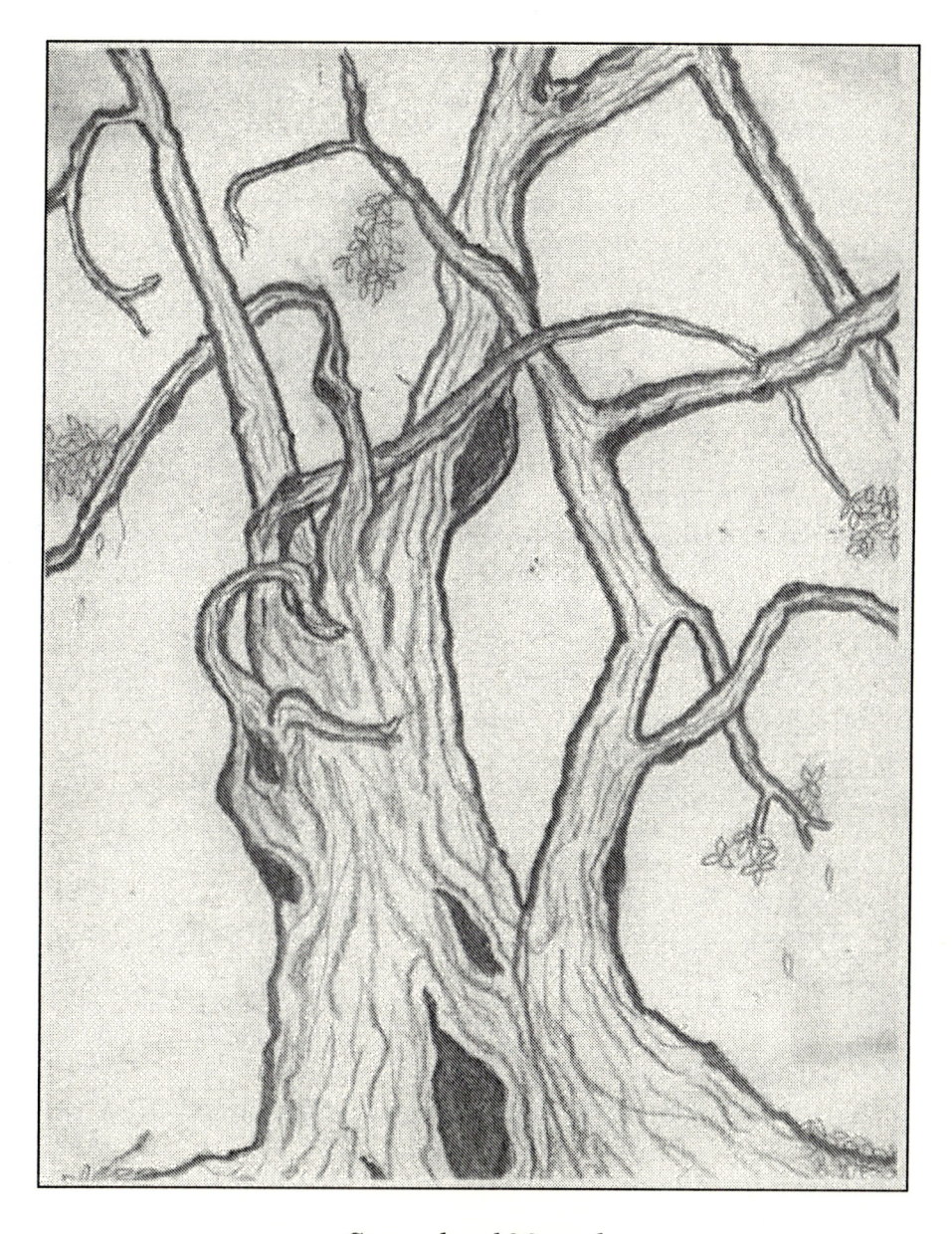

Scarred and Marred

Because

Sometimes we can do nothing more but cry out a desperate prayer to God in an effort to find relief from the overwhelmingly painful emotions pent up inside us. One survivor prayed this:

> *Save me, O God, from myself. Save me from the terrors in my mind, from the hurtful words I tell myself. Deliver me from the demons that roam around in my head, tormenting me night and day. Give my spirit rest, God, please. I can't go one day without thinking about it, without hurting inside, without recognizing the aching chasm deep inside my being. Please help me to forgive. Deliver me from my anger, my resentment, my hate. Let me be satisfied that my questions will remain unanswered, and that even if I knew the answer I wouldn't feel better. I can't take it anymore. This pain that I can't escape is eating me inside. This smile that I wear is only because I'm not allowed to show my feelings. If I did, I would have to explain why I'm depressed. I can't tell anyone. I'm forbidden. Help me God. Please. I'm desperate and I don't know what to do. Sometimes I just want to die; there's a raging scream inside begging to be let out. So many things left unsaid, that will never be said. They are all inside me. My soul hurts so much. I can't just 'get over it.' This has hurt my innermost person, like nothing else has ever hurt before. Every single day I beat myself up about it. Nothing I have is good enough. It never will be. God, why do I feel this way? Why? Please take it away. Make it stop. I'm so sorry for straying so far away. I feel like I'm so far away that I can't ever come back. I feel like I'm at the bottom of a huge pit screaming for help but no sound comes out. No one looks in the pit, or knows I'm there. God, please help me not to hate. Help me to love me for who I am, not what anyone else would have me be. I know You made me this way on purpose, God. You made me, like no one else in the whole world. I am unique. That should matter, shouldn't it? That should comfort me. Why God? I'm going to die if this goes on forever. I need healing but I don't know how to get it. Maybe there is something wrong with me. I know in my head that*

only You can give me healing. God, please help me to believe it in my heart!

In *Search for Significance,* by Robert McGee, we are reminded that love and acceptance are essential needs that each of us possess.

> From life's outset, we find ourselves...searching to satisfy some inner, unexplained yearning. Our hunger causes us to search for people who will love us. Our desire for acceptance pressures us to perform for the praise of others. We strive for success, driving our minds and bodies harder and farther, hoping that because of our sweat and sacrifice, others will appreciate us more (11).

He goes on to explain that when we live only for the love and attention of others we can never be satisfied, nor will we find lasting peace. "Our desire to be loved and accepted is a symptom of a deeper need - the need that often governs our behavior and is the primary source of our emotional pain. This," he goes on to explain, "is our need for self-worth" (11). How then can we assume that the loss of those very things which were necessary for us will not have lasting and sometimes devastating effects upon us? These essentials have been by the very nature of abuse stripped away and a huge gap left in our hearts.

Our desperate search, by whatever means, will keep us dependent upon survival tactics and will so chip away at our personhood that we no longer know who we are or that we are valuable as human beings apart from the conditional approval of others. We will establish unhealthy ways of coping and dysfunctional bonds in relationships as a result.

Betrayal is another deep-rooted issue that every survivor must deal with. Betrayal and duplicity, especially when exhibited by our primary caretakers, are absolutely devastating to the one hurt by them.

Because

Afraid at Night

Diann explains the feelings of betrayal that a child in an abusive situation feels:

> Facing the truth about our abuse is painful and oftentimes gut wrenching. In the case of incest, finding one's own parents guilty of betrayal is a source of soul-scarring pain and grief, to put it mildly. The dictionary defines "betrayal" as *"to lead astray, to deliver to an enemy by treachery, to fail or desert in time of need."* Yet words are in no way sufficient to express the depth of anguish that a child who has been betrayed in this way experiences.

How can anyone adequately express or describe what it feels like knowing that those who should have loved and protected you refused to do so? What do we come to believe about ourselves as a result? What are the consequences of such cruel sin against innocent and powerless victims in such circumstances? Ps. 55:12 and 13 expresses what the psalmist was feeling when he had been betrayed by a friend, but oh how much more when our own family members were our perpetrators!

Another subject that is extremely convoluted for so many of us is shame. It is one of the most difficult and painful issues to work through. *The roots of shame run deep and are excruciatingly painful to extract.* Every survivor struggles with shame, whatever form it takes. Robert McGee wrote these words:

> *"The truth that I am deeply loved, fully pleasing, and totally accepted by the God of the universe has taken me a lifetime to comprehend" (103).*

Why is that? Why is it so much easier to cling to the shame when, seemingly, the simple answer is letting it go? Is the abuse ever a survivor's fault? *Is* it? It cannot be said enough, abuse is never, ever the victim's fault. Why, then, is shame such a strong and destructive byproduct of abuse?

Shame is such a complex emotion. It tenaciously twists its roots around us and refuses to let go no matter what we "know" in our heads. Information, then, is simply not enough to heal it.

What is shame? Shame can be described as a painful feeling of embarrassment or disgrace brought on by doing *(or believing* we are doing) something wrong. It is the result of the humiliation and total lack of honor and regard for the dignity of the one being shamed. It is the lack of honor, honesty, fairness, respect, and being made to feel worthwhile and significant. Yet we need these things that are "proof" to us that we are valuable. They prove to us that we matter. A lack of feeling loved, honored, respected, accepted, will tend to produce the contrary. When we are shame-based, we will find ourselves reacting, rather than responding, to people and situations we encounter in the course of everyday life. Shame can be an insidious companion to travel the road of life with, to say the least.

How do we know if shame is an impediment for us? Consider the following statements and ask yourself, are they true for me?

- There are certain things about my past that I cannot bear to think about without experiencing strong, painful emotions (guilt, shame, anger, fear, etc.).

Because

- There are aspects of me (such as my appearance, habits, behavior, demeanor) that I cannot accept.

- I am disgusted with myself; I hate who I am.

- Because of my past I feel ruined and dirty, worthless and disqualified.

- I feel anxious when I have to make a decision. Making decisions is painful and frightening to me.

- There are things about me that I want to change, but I am convinced that I will fail.

- I will never have a good life because I don't deserve it. I am "damaged goods."

Dr. Dan Allender, in his book *The Wounded Heart,* puts it this way:

> Shame is a result of seeing ourselves as deficient and undesirable by someone whom we hope will care about and love us. Exposure of our (often only perceived) deficiencies leads to feelings of shame...Shame is a dreaded, deep-seated, long-held terror come true: what we have feared has actually come about...All our most elaborate defenses, disguises, and personality traits are held in bondage to the goal of not being known, because to be known is to be caught exposed and defenseless. Much of the shame we experience is not due to the exposure of our sin, but the fear of how we will be perceived as sinful by others (66-67).

He further explains the difference between illegitimate and legitimate shame:

> When our dignity is ignored or demeaned, we will feel exposed as undesirable, and we will likely hate whatever part of us has caused the pain - but the part of ourselves we hate even more is our longing to be wanted and enjoyed. We feel

shame when our longings surface and we are failed or we fail. A godly response in the face of abuse is to grieve - for the perpetrator's sin and for the damage done to our soul; but the natural response is to cower in shame, condemning ourselves for being so foolish as to hope, want, or risk. Illegitimate shame comes when we have failed to achieve what our heart craves (the longings that reflect our dignity) and we feel we are at fault, because if we had not done...then we would not feel empty, alone, and exposed. Legitimate shame always leads to a sense of being lifted up *by God to possess what is surprising...and undeserved (69)*.

What are the effects of shame?

Allender and others discuss many of the effects of shame with which survivors are shackled. John Bradshaw's *Healing The Shame That Binds You* also discusses the effects of "toxic shame" at length. This discussion of the effects of shame is by no means all-inclusive or exclusive. You may find yourself struggling beneath effects not covered here, or you may only experience some of the following. Regardless, it is important to take hold of the truth that shame is not heaped upon us by God, it is from the enemy. Part of the healing process includes replacing shame with appropriate guilt; guilt righteously placed on those who deserve it - the perpetrators, not on the innocent victims.

Ambivalence

According to Dr. Allender, "ambivalence is the emotional battle with two (or more) minds, wills, and desires...it is feeling two contrary energies moving us in opposite directions, being caught in the bind of opposing desires, feeling divided and torn." Because we "feel shame when we feel stripped of control" the struggle in decision-making can become overwhelmingly intense (143).

Habitually Self Destructive Behavior

Because

Seeing ourselves through the eyes of shame usually results in a pessimistic outlook on life and a lifestyle of destructive behavior. Our shame, however, forbids us to become angry with anyone else, therefore we take our anger and frustration out on the safest person to be angry with - ourselves.

Self Pity

Our "victim mentality" causes us to blame others or ourselves for our actions and we sink into the depths of despair because we believe there really is no way out.

Passivity

Refusing to invest any part of ourselves in relationships and responsibilities. Perfection and other unhealthy (unbalanced) behaviors drive us so that we are "too busy" to experience the reality of relationships and situations.

Isolation and Withdrawal

We avoid both the risks of rejection and failure or withdraw from meaningful interaction. We develop facades so that nobody can see our hurt. We don't allow anyone to get close to us. Our deep sense of shame leads us to withdraw from others, feel isolated, and experience the pain of loneliness.

Loss of Creativity

When we experience shame over a period of time, the cutting edge of our creativity atrophies. We tend to become so preoccupied with our own inferiority that we are unable to come up with new ideas.

Codependent Relationships

In an attempt to overcome their sense of shame, many people become codependent; that is, they depend on being needed by a family member or friend who has an addictive problem or compulsion. Codependents thus develop a need to "rescue" and take care of others. This care taking is the codependent's subconscious way of trying to gain personal significance. Such attempts usually backfire, however, because frequently, dependent persons often use shame to manipulate the codependent. 'Codas' fall prey to frequent ploys where they are made to feel guilty for taking care of personal needs and affairs rather than those of the dependent person. This locks the coda into a hopeless pattern of rescuing to gain approval and then feeling shamed because of their inability to develop a sense of personal value regardless of how hard he or she tries to do so.

Contempt for others

Shame will cause us to tend to turn to contempt of others in order to hide our feelings of guilt and inadequacy. Self-contempt is a sure sign that we are contemptuous of others' imperfections. We certainly will love others as we love ourselves, whether we are aware of this truth, or not.

Shame can be so overwhelmingly painful that we will do almost anything to numb ourselves from those realities of its sources. Eating disorders and the like often have a shame component to them, as well. This is, obviously, no small issue.

What is the Solution?

Robert McGee, in his book *Search For Significance,* offers an important aspect of healing from shame: Regeneration. He writes, "this is not a self-improvement program, nor is it a clean-up campaign for our sinful natures. Regeneration is nothing less than the impartation of new life" (110). Renewal comes by spiritual rebirth that can only be found in the Creator and Giver of life, Jesus Christ. This, like everything else in life, is a process. Rom. 12:2 talks about being transformed by the renewing of our minds. Renewing takes time. New experiences, new and healthier encounters with life and people will help that transformation to occur.

Now let's look at the issue of trust. Why is this such an incredibly huge issue for abuse survivors? The question seems to be obvious, but it isn't. At times, even we cannot understand our own lack of

Because

ability to trust - whether it be placing our trust in God or anyone else. Why is that?

Some synonyms for trust are faith, confidence, conviction, hope, belief, reliance, dependence, expectation. For someone who has been abused, these things were obviously missing! Surrounded by an atmosphere of unpredictability on a regular basis sows roots of distrust that are too deep to extricate without much time and concentrated effort. Is it any wonder, then, that trust is so difficult to achieve?

Let's ask ourselves first what trust is. Trust is experienced when the freedom to have confidence in those we ought to be able to look to for provision and safety are doing their part. Trust doesn't always come naturally, it is earned. Remember that commercial of the little boy afraid to take his first leap into the water? His father stands in front of him, ready to catch him in his strong arms and help him stay afloat until he learns to swim. What would happen to a child who is promised safety and allowed to sink at the same time? He certainly wouldn't be willing to jump in as easily next time!

When trust is betrayed we become fearful, afraid of taking chances again because the consequence of betrayed trust is such a painful thing to have to bear. When our life experiences have taught us that nothing and no one is predictable, not even ourselves, we will live life constantly disappointed, though we often mistakenly believe that withholding all trust protects us.

Because so many of us have been shamed for our lack of trust, we need to dwell on this point for a moment. While we will hear differing opinions as to how to go about "learning" to trust, we need to look to the scriptures for the best source of guidance in this area. Let's look at Jesus, then, as a model of trust. Did He imprudently put His trust in people just to prove He was emotionally stable and healthy? Jesus was selective about where and with whom He entered into a trust relationship. He "knew what was in man," (which was a wonderful advantage we simply cannot accurately have). He was wise. He looked for fruit and in some cases waited for fruit to mature.

As John 2:25 (and many other such verses) illustrates, He didn't have the same level of interaction in every relationship.

The word of God never tells us to put our trust in man, but in God alone. *"Trust in **THE LORD**,"* we are reminded in the scriptures again and again (Ps. 37:3, Ps. 118:8, Prov. 3:5, etc.). We must start there, the rest will follow.

Does this mean that we who struggle with this issue of trust should not work on growing in this area? It doesn't mean that at all, but since God patiently gives us the freedom to work out these issues, so must we graciously allow one another the same kindness. He doesn't shame us for not being able to give what we cannot. He doesn't force us to trust even Him, not even when it's for our good. It's because He proves His love and trustworthiness to us again and again that we come to love and trust Him in return. He is altogether worthy of our trust, and that's why we *can* trust Him. It is upon His example and foundation that trust within relationships can then be built.

Now here is the crux of the matter for many of us, and we must consider it: can **God** be trusted? *Can* God be trusted? How can we know? After all, the enemy stands day and night loudly accusing Him to us, and accusing us to Him. The conclusion? *Some*body is lying! The decision as to whom we will believe is ours alone. Because we have a free will, we must come to our own resolution as to who we will and will not believe, whom we will and will not serve. *God will not, even for our own good, charge down from heaven and force us to choose, believe, or do the right thing.* It is entirely up to us then. He has given us the tools, but we must utilize them. Whom *will* we choose?

Let's think carefully about this question: Why should *I* trust Him? Where will I turn for my source of Truth? If the Word of God is truly my standard of truth then I must turn there for the answers, first and foremost.

For those of us who struggle with some of these issues, here are a few more "becauses" to consider:

Because

Because God *cannot* lie (Titus 1:2).

Because of Who He has revealed Himself to be in His Word.

Because of Who Jesus is, and who He has exposed Satan to be (the deceiver, liar, imposter, usurper, thief, murderer, destroyer, accuser, and more!), *and because He has overcome him,* we **do** have a choice.

Because God is our Healer, Helper, Counselor, Creator, King, Restorer, and because He has sent His Son to be our Savior, Lord, Redeemer, Advocate, Example, Teacher, Shepherd, Hope, Light, Salvation, and because His Holy Spirit is our Comforter, Interpreter, Guide, Quickener, Sanctifier, Witness, Empowerer, Illuminator, because of this, and so much more, everything has changed!

Because He is complete, and He is in us, we are complete in Him. We *do* have all that we need to live the life that God Himself deeply longs for us to have. Phil 4:19, Heb 4:16, etc., etc. Because of what Jesus did, everything's changed. The rules have changed. I have hope.

> *"According as **His** divine power hath given unto us **all things** that pertain unto life and godliness, **through** the knowledge of him that hath called us to glory and virtue"*
> *II Pet. 1:3*

"Because He is at my right hand, I shall not be moved!" the psalmist confidently exults (Ps. 16:8). No one, not even the enemy of our souls, can snatch us out of His strong hand. No matter what has happened in our lives, God has never forgotten us (Isa. 49:16), and He will surely redeem our pain and restore our desolation (Jer. 15:21, 30:17). There is such incredible hope! Neither the will of man nor Satan's influence can change the good will and divine intention God has for our lives. When all is said and done, God's will <u>will</u> prevail! We can have confidence that, no matter how things look from our very finite point of view, He will do all that He has said He will do. He is and will do all that He promised.

He is Jehovah Shammah - Ever Present, there (Mt. 1:23, Isa. 9:6, Ps 139:7, Mt.28:20)
He is Jehovah Rophe - our Healer (Ex. 15:26, Ps. 103:3, Isa. 58:8, Jer. 30:17)
He is Jehovah Shalom - our Peace (Jdg. 6:24, Eph. 2:14, Phil. 4:7)
He is Jehovah Jireh - our Provider (Gen. 22:8, Phil. 4:19)
He is Jehovah Nissi - our Banner (Ex. 17:15, I Cor. 15:57)
He is Jehovah M'Kaddesh - our Sanctification (Zeph. 3:17, Jn. 17:17)
He is Jehovah Rohi - our Shepherd (Jn. 10:14, Ps. 34:10)
He is Jehovah Tsidkenu - our Righteousness (Jer. 23:6, I Cor. 1:30, Ps. 71:16)
He is El Shaddai - our All Sufficient One (II Cor. 3:5, 12:9,10)
He is our Hope (Col. 1:27, I Tim. 1:1, Ps. 18:28, Ps. 38:15)
He is our Redeemer (Job 19:25, Ps. 19:14, Isa. 62:12)
He is our Helper and Deliverer (I Chron. 15:4, 20:15, Ps. 50:15, 143:9, Jer. 31:11)
He is our Restorer (Isa. 57:18, Ps 23:3, Joel 2:25, Eze. 36:33-36)
He is our Comfort (Ps. 94:19, Isa. 57:18, 19)
He is our Salvation (Hab. 3:18, Lk. 1:47, Ps. 18:1-3, Acts 4:12)
He is our Confidence (Ps. 71:5, I Jn. 3:20,21)
He is our Strong Tower (Ps. 61:3, Prov. 18:10)
He is our Sun and our Shield (Ps. 84:11, Jn.17:11)
He is our Rock, our Strength (Ps. 31:3, I Cor. 10:4, Ex. 15:2, Ps. 18:1, 59:9)
He is our Purpose and Reason (II Tim. 1:9, Rom. 8:28)
He is our Hiding Place and Refuge (Ps. 32:7, Isa. 4:6, Ps 46:1, 11, Deu. 33:27, Isa. 32:7)
He is our Light (Isa. 60:19, 20, Ps. 27:1)
He is our Abiding Place (Jn. 15:1,5)
He is our Justification (Rom. 5:18, 8:1)
He is our Life (Rom. 8:11, Act. 17:28)
He is our Shade and Shelter (Ps. 121:5, Isa. 25:4)
He is Alpha and the Omega, the Beginning and the End of all things! (Rev. 21:6, 22:13)

Best of all, God being God is not dependent upon me, upon my gifting, my strengths, my good deeds, nor upon my level of faith. *He*

Because

changes not, no matter what (Heb. 13:8). It's not about me; it's not about my righteousness or my ability to save or redeem; it's about His. Because He has said, *"I will never leave thee nor forsake thee"* we can *boldly* and gladly and joyfully and confidently proclaim, *"The LORD is my helper!"(Heb. 13:6).* It is good news that He is sufficient, for I will never be, but He is enough, and I don't have to be! Good news indeed!

What will we do with such wonderful knowledge and truth? It is for each one of us to decide, individually and on a deeply personal level. But because we *can* choose we *must* choose Who will be Lord in our lives. Why must we choose? Because when we live life contrary to what we feel or believe we become anxious and discouraged and overwhelmed and depressed. We must take hold of, then, our freedom to choose. No one can, nor do they have the right, to do that for us, nor to insist that we come to the same conclusions they have in the same way they have. Sometimes we can't have all the answers we want before making a choice. Sometimes the only choice is life with, or without, God. As for me, I chose God, and have never regretted it.

"He is my Lord and I will wait for Him, my God, and I will exalt Him" (Ex. 15:2).

The Eagle Story

We were at our weekly Bible study group one Thursday night when one of the women shared a story she had heard during a sermon. As she recounted it, we all became excited at the thought of how God, like the mother eagle, teaches us to fly.

> *"As an eagle stirs up her nest, hovers over her young, spreads her wings to catch them, and carries them on her wings..." (Deut. 32:11 NAS).*

Many of us, however, just like the young eaglets, are afraid of the learning process and would rather stay in the safety of the nest! The mother eagle has a "cure" for this problem, though. Nests are built with sticks and other sharp materials, and then lined with leaves and soft animal fur. While the eaglets are small the nest is a comfortable place to be nurtured and kept safe, but as the eaglets grow and are old enough to learn to fly the soft lining is moved aside so that remaining in the nest beyond the proper time becomes quite uncomfortable. This encourages the eaglets to perch on the side of the nest so that "flight training" can begin.

I have read a couple of accounts of what happens next; either the mother eagle pushes the eaglets over the side, or she actually picks them up and drops them so that they will *have* to use their God given abilities.

From my perspective, I can only imagine what that's like based on my own experiences in the "learning to fly process" - looking down (YIKES!), panicking at the prospect of the drop, finding myself unwillingly airborne, not having a clue what to do next, more panicking, flapping wildly, expecting disaster and total annihilation…but then suddenly, like the eaglet being caught by the strong parent eagle beneath, I am once again rescued, saved from (but for my Father's intervention) sure death! And just like that eagle who returns his young to the nest so that the process can start all over again, and again, until the eagle learns to do what it is created to do, so God the Father returns me to the learning place. He doesn't want me to miss out on doing the very thing that I, too, was created to do - soar on mighty wings like an eagle with incredible grace and swiftness! And you know what? Neither do I! It's so exciting to be in the process with God, of coming to the realization that the Creator of the universe and all that it contains is that committed to my healing and growth. I am so deeply grateful for that, and cannot but stand in awe of His incredible confidence in His ability to bring me through it all.

"Hast thou not known? Hast thou not heard? That the everlasting God, the Lord, the Creator of the ends of the earth, faints not, neither grows weary. There is no searching of His understanding. He gives power to the faint, and to them that have no might He increases strength. Even the youths shall faint and be weary, and the young

Because

men shall utterly fall, but they that wait upon the Lord shall renew their strength; they shall mount up with wings as eagles; they shall run, and not be weary; and they shall walk, and not faint"
(Isa. 40:28-31 KJV).

Why does the darkness even come at all? Why must evil prevail? Why was man given a free will if it would be used to hurt and destroy? Why is the enemy allowed to wreak such damage and destruction and pain? There are no clear answers for some of these things, at least not here, not now. Why, then, do we waste precious time and energy trying to control things we simply cannot? Why waste so much time fruitlessly allowing the enemy to run us around in circles chasing after what we cannot catch? Why not *instead* turn our eyes upon Him Who knows all things and Who alone can judge when and how best to deal with them? Our part is so much simpler than that! We simply need to show up, God does the rest when we invite Him to do so. *"Come unto Me…and I will."*

*"He who dwells in the secret place of the Most High shall **rest, remain stable and fixed** under the shadow of the Almighty (Whose power no foe can withstand). I will say of the Lord, **He** is my refuge and my fortress; my God, **on Him** will I lean and rely, and in Him will I confidently trust! Surely **He** shall deliver you from the snare of the fowler, **He** shall cover you with His pinions, and under His wings shall you trust and find refuge; **His** Truth and faithfulness are a shield and buckler…because you have made the Lord, which is my refuge, even the most High, your dwelling place."*

*"Because he hath set his love upon Me, therefore **will I deliver** him; **I will set** him on high, because he hath known My Name. He shall call upon Me, and **I will answer** him: **I will be with** him in trouble; **I will deliver** him, and honor him. With long life **will I satisfy** him, and **show** him My salvation" (Ps. 91:1-4, 14-16 Amp).*

Letters

Things we wish we could say...

In this section we'd like to share one more bit of our hearts. We'd like to express on paper what we could not, and often still cannot, express in audible words.

I feel so worthless

How has abuse affected the way we view ourselves? How has it affected our ability to communicate clearly what it feels like inside? Our lives have been touched by so many people! Each of those people have had an affect on us, one way or another. As we continue our walk through this life, whether it be in the deep shadows of the nighttime or in the full light of day, we will affect one another for good or for not so good. We will leave a mark, often a lasting one that has the potential to transform the way we will perceive life as a result of that mark. Our hope is that each of us will be impressed enough to make a difference for good in the lives of those we come in contact with. Perhaps one way this can be accomplished is through honest communication. In this section, then, we have included some letters we have written, most unsent, but at least putting into written words the things that are upon our hearts and minds.

Letters

A Letter to my family
from Laura

I want to tell you a story. Once upon a time, a blind lobster took up residence with a clown fish. The lobster kept the burrow neat and clean and, in exchange for the homemaking, the clown fish warned of any approaching predators. The lobster kept an antennae on the fish at all times, so she could feel the physical changes in the fish since her eyes couldn't see for themselves. In this way, the lobster placed all responsibility for her well being on the fish. That the fish was also a predator was of little or no concern to the lobster - as long as she was taken care of.

Now the clown fish was born with the ability to hide his hideous nature behind the funny stripes painted on his face. Out of all the creatures, he could have taken up residence with anyone he chose. He chose the lobster, knowing she was blind and dependent upon him to take care of her physical safety and needs. As soon as the fish's body became tense or ridged, the lobster retreated to the safety of the dark burrow where the lack of sight didn't matter.

Now, in time, the two sea creatures had children. The first child was beautiful. She had the beautiful stripes of the clown fish and the form of the lobster. But the most stunning part of her were her eyes. They were violet and sighted. As this child grew and saw the nature of the fish, she tried hiding. The lobster couldn't help, as she was blind and didn't see what was happening. And so, the first child became a target of the fish's violent nature. When the second child was born she looked very much like the lobster. Her eyes were not violet, but they could see. As time passed, the second child saw the violent nature of the fish as he targeted and mistreated the older child. She saw how the efforts of the older child to communicate the offenses to the lobster were met with indifference and disbelief.

In time, the second child learned to be meek so as not to also become a target of the fish's violent nature. The most terrifying part of life for the second child was when night came. During the daylight she could see where the danger came from, but at night, the terror came to her and crept into her dreams. By now, the older child had taken on the violent nature of the clown fish. She had learned that, in order to survive, she had to be able to make herself look very big and very mean. She learned to strike at everything that came close to her. Her stripes were helpful as they identified the power of the clown fish yet her form was that of the lobster and made her vulnerable.

The second child, having no stripes, had nothing that indicated power or danger to others. She learned that her form made her vulnerable to predators and so, although she could see, she learned to retreat. She also learned to keep her mouth shut, as communicating to the blind lobster had no effect.

Time went by in this way and two more children were born. The third child had the form of the lobster with very faint stripes. She was blind. The fourth had the form of the fish but without the stripes. He had the temperament of the lobster and was also blind.

The second child grew up believing that she was unique and misplaced. Her form was the same as the blind lobster and the two other lobster children, but she wasn't blind and she didn't have stripes. She only saw the differences, not the similarities, and she set out to pretend to be like the others, not realizing that the secret…

I can't write anymore. I guess you get the idea.

Letters

A letter to my grandfather
from Robyn

"Grandfather." What a joke that title is. What a joke you were; never a grandfather, someone to turn to in times of trouble. You were the trouble.

You did an awfully good job of making me believe I was worthless and the cause of all your problems, especially the ones you had with my mother.

You had a perverse pride in letting me know I wasn't wanted, in telling me that my mother should have aborted me. After all, it's easier to live with the sorrow of what might have been (where I could have been anything in your mind) rather than the day-to-day reality of who and what I really was.

You weren't alone, not even you had this much power. Your wife was a very large key in the equation. She used you for the muscle, the underlying threat of pain if I didn't do what she wanted. What a pair you two were. She still tries to evoke loyalty by conjuring your name.

Then, of course, there is the issue of sexual abuse. I don't remember much of it, but I do have some flashes. Your penis in my mouth. Lying naked on the bathroom floor while grandmother squeezed the ball that delivered the enema while you watched from the doorway. What did you feel watching that? Did it excite you? Did it make you feel powerful? What a pathetic piece of crap you were.

You were very thorough in tearing down my self-esteem; I'm sure you were very proud of yourself.

***********************BUT************************

Just Before Dawn

NO MORE!!!! I have been shown by Jesus just how much I am loved. How much He cares; that He will <u>never</u> hurt me. That He will never leave me; that even if my mother and father and grandparents would forsake me (and they did), He wouldn't. He showed me that I was chosen by Him, before the beginning of the earth. He has shown me that you were wrong! Wrong, wrong, wrong. HA! I am loved! I am wanted! God delights in me! I am His child and I never need to worry that He won't love me or care for me or leave me.

He has also shown me that I don't have to waste my time hating you and wishing you punishment because God will mete out your punishment; He will call my account into balance. You will pay for your evil acts at His hand because He knows everything. He will act as my advocate and make sure all accounts are paid in full.

Knowing all of this and knowing that you will be subjected to the scrutiny of God Almighty Himself means that I can almost feel sorry for you. I can allow myself to forgive you because your soul has a much larger adversary than me. I can't tell you how much peace that knowledge brings me.

Letters

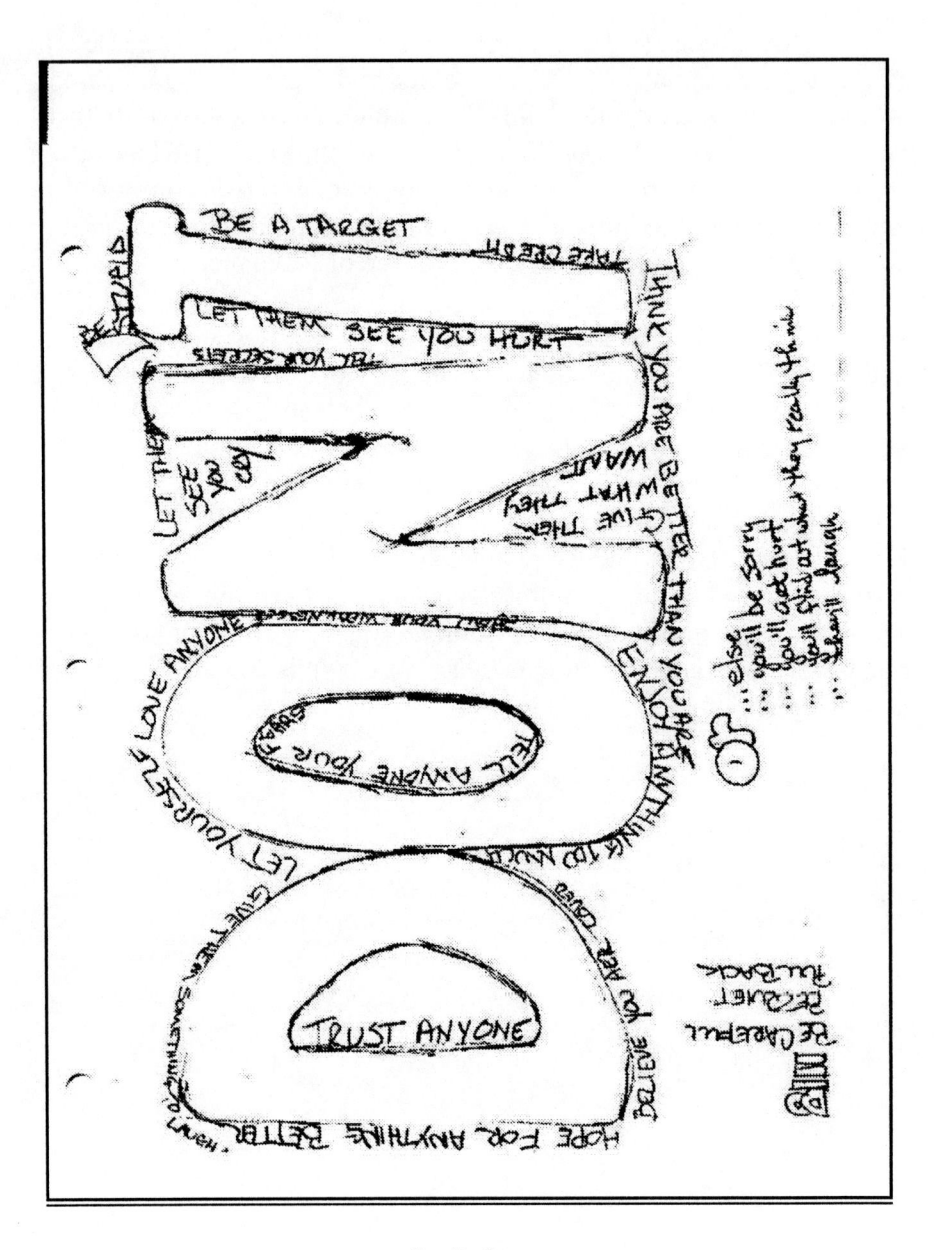

By Robyn

A letter to Paula, my counselor
from Beth

I was the sobbing young girl on the opposite couch
The small little engine who never thought she could
The pathetic, lost, despondent little grouch

You were the eyes who never judged and always understood
The ears who listened faithfully, deciphered all my tears
The smile when I told you that I didn't know my mood

You helped me through my last four years
Never turned away my urgent calls
Always subsided my foolish fears

You've helped me through each of my pitfalls
Never labeled my problems as inane
Patiently helped me to tear down these walls

You've been there for much: friends that were a pain
When I didn't want to live, when I didn't want to die,
Don't forget that boyfriend who was insane

One good thing resulted from that psychotic control freak full of lies
If not for him, I would never have met you, or you me
He urged me to seek counsel; at least in one way he was wise

I bet he never figured that you would help me see
His freakish nature and tell me then was the time to elude it
I think of his demise and smile; is this malignancy?

My smile grows to think that you became to me mommy number two
You're my favorite grown-up (besides of course, mommy number one)
Thanks for what you are to me, you helped make my life brand new

Letters

Thanks for brightening my one time dreary sun
For seeing me to that very distant end
For bringing me to the other side, helping me have fun again
Thanks for not just being my counselor, but one of my best friends.

I love you, I love you.

A Letter to my doctor
from Lexy

Dear Dr.——,

I wanted to write and tell you some things that I can never seem to explain to you when I make an appointment to see you. What I experience when I come to your office is very different from what most of your patients experience. I thought that, if I explained what happens to me when I come to see you, it might help us both, and some other patients, too.

You see, doctor, I am a survivor of childhood abuse. I often need to see you because the trauma I suffered in the past still has physical effects on me in the present. For example, sometimes I am not able to sleep because of the nightmares and flashbacks that still haunt me. There are times I suffer insomnia for weeks on end, and I want to ask you for something to help me sleep. When I see you, though, I never seem able to express these things to you clearly. Then I worry that you and your staff might have labeled me a hypochondriac because I have come in for no apparent reason. I have wanted to explain why this happens but get tongue tied when I try.

This sounds silly, coming from a grown woman with an education, a career, and a "good" life, but I crumble in the face of authority; I freeze and become intimidated. You may not feel that you are intimidating, but your office and the position of doctor is. Often, the abuse I suffered was blamed on me and I was told that it was necessary to "make me better." Making me better - isn't that what doctors do? I hope you see the connection.

Medical settings in general are very frightening for me. When I sit in your office, having dutifully had my arm squeezed by the blood pressure cuff (and having tried not to flash back to hurtful hands doing the same thing), I see all of those instruments you have around. I study each one and wonder what pain you are going to need to inflict on me with one of them. I see the anatomy models you have of organs. The heart one bothers me most. I saw a still-beating heart in the body of a dying woman before I was old enough to even know what a heart did. I see the used needles through the plastic of the sharps disposal container; I try not to think about the times needles were used to "teach me to behave." I sit and I wait for you, surrounded by all of these links to the terror with which I was raised.
I wonder if your staff is laughing at me, talking about how I have another appointment because I just "think" I'm ill and that the time I'm taking up should be given to someone with a legitimate infirmity. This is what I think and feel before you enter the room.

When you walk in, I instantly feel six again. I am the small child in the doctor's office who is severely ill, but cannot tell the doctor why. It would break the rules to tell the doctor that my tummy started hurting after my dad raped me. I would get hurt worse for breaking the rules, so I suffered through barium enemas, intestinal analyses, and strict diets which were formulated to help me with this terrible "mysterious" pain I had in my abdomen. That's what I think of when you ask me what the trouble is. Complaining or telling you what I really feel is breaking the rules, even now.

I am ashamed to tell you that I can't sleep. I am ashamed to tell you that I have severe pelvic pain, although all of the ultrasounds are negative. I am ashamed to tell you about my migraines, and ashamed to ask for something to bring some relief. I feel that I am a whining baby who brought all of this pain on myself; if I could just, "take it like a big girl," then I wouldn't be here in your office. But I am here. And I need your help. The problem is that I need your help to be able

Letters

to ask you to help me. I need to know that it's OK to ask you to help me. I need to know that you aren't going to hurt me needlessly. I need to know that you believe me when I say I have pain and that you will help me to fix it, not just tell me to "live with it" or "not think" about it.

When you try to examine me, I need you to explain to me what you are going to do. I need you to tell me you are going to touch me, push on me, twist me, and why you are going to do this. Please don't just poke me in the abdomen and ask if it hurts without telling me what you are doing; too many people have done that to me just to make me hurt and expected me not to complain. Please understand that I have been through hell and survived, but that the "old rules" still bind me more than I like. Please ask if anything ever happened which could complicate my health; I can't tell you about being little and being given douches of bleach if you don't let me know that it's OK to tell you this. I'm afraid that you will wonder what a filthy little girl I was to need such treatment; this keeps me from telling you about it, even though I have so many problems which are probably caused by this.

Most of all, I need you to listen to me and watch me when I talk. When I was on a different table, with a different set of shiny, sharp things coming at me, I would stare at something until I wasn't so aware of what was being done to my body. That was the only way I could handle the pain they inflicted, which is so much like the discomfort of so many medical tests. When you perform your tests, I often "go away". Then, when you talk to me about treatment or diagnosis, I am not really there. Please ask me to respond and make sure I understand. Please ask me to repeat what you have said. Please don't rush out of the room like I'm some sort of leper or some person who is wasting your time. Realize that this is hard for me, please; realize that I need your help, but that your help terrifies me because of what it reminds me of.

They say that the hair of the dog that bit you is the best medicine. When I come to see you, that's exactly what I fear. I come to you for help from the scars of abuse, but medicine seems like more abuse sometimes. Please let me know that you see me as a person, not a problem. Please try not to have me wait so long in the room with the terrifying tools. Please put the models and diagrams of organs away when you aren't using them as aids to talk to patients. Please tell me that it's safe to tell you things; let me know that you won't laugh at me, judge me, or call me a liar. Most of all, please listen to me and respond so that I can finally have some of the pain end by gaining some physical healing.

A letter to my dentist
from Karen

Dear Dr. C.,

It's me again. You know, the one that was in there last week to get another tooth repaired. I'm the one that always panics when the chair starts to tip backward. Remember how I sit up straight while it slowly falls back into that laying down position? That's the one part that triggers me the most, so I make sure that I lay down myself rather than letting that chair tip me back that way. Even after all these years, it is still so hard to not find myself back in that place in my mind where the worst memories are of how they hurt me in a way that seems too similar to being in a dentist's chair. The light above me and the shiny things coming at my face terrify that part of me inside that remembers it, though I try very hard to keep such memories deep, deeply hidden away from even my conscious mind and thoughts.

I was around 14 when they did that. That was the day I made the lady in charge of the girls too mad. She said I had to be taught to obey without question; no speaking allowed. Now I had to pay the price. Time to get hurt again. It was something long and shiny with a hook on the end. They held me down from both sides so I couldn't get away. They held my shoulders down and my head still and someone forced open my mouth. I am absolutely petrified of shiny things

Letters

coming at my face. Needles I hate, especially the ones that only hurt without medicine in them that helps.

How could anyone hate any other human being so much that they would do and say to them the things they did to me? I believed it, too. I hated it. I hated her. I hated the pain. But mostly I hated me - for breaking the rules, for speaking when no one wanted to hear, for thinking that standing up for what I wanted or felt mattered enough to take a dumb chance like that.

And I paid for it, too.
Like my dad used to say, you just always have to learn the hard way. Well, I've come a long way since then, though some things are still very ingrained in my belief system. I just keep working on it a day at a time, and it's getting better, really.

You asked me last time if I'd ever put some of my experiences in writing. The answer is that I'm beginning to. I'm trying to find my voice still, but that's a process, too. This piece of writing is for you, because you had the kindness to ask - like you cared, or as if it mattered. For that, I thank you.

I thank you, too, for your incredible patience over the years that I have been coming there. Your gentle manner has helped me to heal from some of those old fears, and for those on your staff who know "something happened" and have been so kind I send my thankful appreciation, as well.

A Letter to God

Dear God,

I had to write you this letter because these things just can't be said out loud...

Just Before Dawn

First, I need to tell you that I'm so broken! I guess You know that already, but I just need to say it to someone. Everything inside me hurts. It's like being in a thousand little pieces, and I'm too fragmented to think clearly enough to fix it. Who will help me? Who will understand this and show me the way back to being just one? Sometimes I think it's too late, that it's too hard even for You. Is it? When You look inside me, do You see it all? All the little pieces my heart and mind have been broken into...

I'm hurt and frustrated by so many things that I just don't understand. I'm filled with questions that don't seem to have an answer. Even though I've come so far, I never seem to be able to get to that apparently nonexistent place of rest and acceptance that all people seem to long for. So maybe I'm not so strange, right?

Here's the problem:
Right now I am mad.
Mad because there is so much suspicion in the body of Christ,
Mad because it is never safe to trust enough to let your guard down,
Mad because it is not fair to have to live and function this way.
Just mad.
Mad because I have done so much work and have accomplished so much and yet
that is not good enough,
I am not good enough.

I am discouraged at the enormity of the task before me,
and the realization that it just may always be that in the eyes of many people
I will never quite measure up,
I will always be suspect,
my motives and intentions will always be questioned
and food for thought in people's minds.
I will always be an oddity to others
And never quite fit.
I am sad.

Letters

Dear God,
I don't fit.
How often I've wished
for a place to belong
to be accepted
for who I really am
to be wanted
no strings attached
to feel cared for
safe
secure.

As I've grown
I find I no longer fit in old molds
but am not quite accepted into new ones.
Trust is hard
believing almost impossible
resting alludes me.

Dear God,
I cannot make me fit.
Only one place feels right,
a perfectly sculpted out hiding place:
The cleft in the Rock.
Hidden there
I am no longer afraid,
though I long, at times,
for something here.

Now I wait upon You
and will wait.
Only help me be still
And patient
Keep me looking upward
And hoping
in you alone.

A letter to myself

Sometimes I still feel like crying.
I used to be told that the past shouldn't matter, that if I had faith I would just do what Paul did and "forget what lieth behind." Guess I wasn't very good at that then.
Now that things are better it seems, at least to some, that it shouldn't be that way, either, that I shouldn't feel like that anymore.
But I do. Sometimes, it still hurts.
And some days, I just need to grieve the losses.
I feel like one who has a story to tell,
but there's no one to tell it to -
either because I fear their reaction,
or disbelief, or total lack of interest, or whatever.
I'm supposed to be "over all that stuff by now" anyway, my time for grieving has passed.
But can I ever really forget? Could anyone?
I still am afraid, too, of being shamed or hurt or humiliated again.
I am afraid that I will remember the pain and feel it too intensely.
What if the memories become too much to bear again?
Sometimes I wish I could still cry about some of the things that happened…
It's been years now since I first began working on healing from my abuse.
I'm not in counseling anymore.
Now I am the one who counsels others,
I am the one who comes alongside those who are hurting,
who are reeling from the devastating effects of the horrors perpetrated against them.
Now I'm the one who's ok (at least most of the time),
who's traveled the healing path,
who's dealt with the pain, the trauma,
and has moved on to a level of health and wholeness that I at one time in my life seriously doubted was possible.
I've been there, I understand it.

Letters

And I'm honestly glad for the long way You've brought me.
But some days, I feel the old familiar twinge of sadness…
Surprised at the presence of it,
wondering where it came from and why,
and I know that if I stopped long enough to really dwell on it for very long,
I might just possibly cry.
Why this?
Why now?
Would anyone understand?
Why is it not allowed?
I know my husband admires the long way I have come,
All the hard work to get to recovery.
But sometimes I get the message that in his eyes
I will always be suspect,
I will never be "normal" enough,
that my scars will always be unacceptable.
and a reminder, proof against me,
that I was so wounded once upon a time…
I will never be allowed to forget how miserable I used to be,
and how that misery invaded everyone's life,
and that the resentment they feel is justified…
I understand it, but
it's such a heavy burden to bear, and it's not based on reason.
That's just the way things are.
But I still wish I could cry, at least sometimes.

The Invitation

Long time I waited for it
praying it would come.
In my mind's eye, I saw what I would do when it did…
I prepared for it,
saved for it,
spent any bit I could in making sure I had all I might need to
be ready
just in case it did.

Just Before Dawn

*I dreamed of what it would be like
to play a part in that grand scheme of things...
to not feel ever outside looking in
longing and wishing to be good enough to belong.
I imagined myself not just tolerated
but truly wanted, accepted,
Invited.
Every now and then vague allusions to the Invitation were mentioned
and I dared to hope for a while
but apparently it was like the proverbial carrot dangling just out of reach...
for when I looked for the actual coming to pass
the "mailbox" was empty.
I wondered often if perhaps those who held the Invitations had seen something unworthy in me
and changed their minds.
Perhaps I was not wise enough or witty enough or good enough company or
Perhaps I really was not dressed up enough to fit in and attend?
They must behold some stain on my garments
that I do not see
or think that they are too frayed and worn...
I confess they are not as new and preserved as most
but does not the Maker of them all
look rather within
at the heart of the wearer and not so outwardly?
What if I am being foolish or presuming too much?
I am afraid.
Trying to figure it all out I become confused and doubting
and sad and discouraged
and ashamed.*

*Perhaps I will only be allowed
from a distance.
Perhaps the Invitation will not come from them at all.
Let it be enough, then, Lord*

Letters

*that I know Thee
and see Thee in the hidden places only.
Let it be enough that I have Thy company and companionship.
Help me be content
even if I cannot be a part of the music or lift my voice with the worshippers or dance with the others who are glad...*

*O cause me to look up to Thee and remember and rejoice that You invited me to Yourself long time ago.
Thank You, O how I gratefully and with all my heart thank You...and
I accept!*

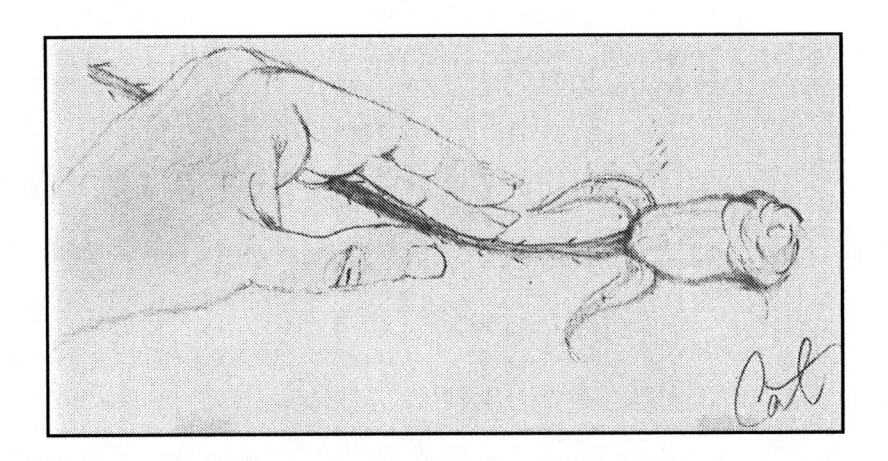

By Catherine

Kicking the Walls

"Behold, thy walls are continually before Me."
Isaiah 49:16

I saw tears in the eyes of the person sitting across from me as I recounted only little bits and pieces of my abuse. I was confused. What had I said wrong? Did I say too much? It was the first time anyone ever actually cried for me. I was completely confounded – I had no idea what to do with such a reaction. Of course, I had never told anyone about my past before, never let anyone know my internal pain, struggles, condition. I felt distressed and ashamed and fearful. I immediately became silent.

"It's the walls," she said sadly. I think I understood, even back then. The walls surrounding me were so high, so intact, so incredibly fortified...Looking back now, it makes me sad, too, that for so long I lived all alone with my pain, and that I believed that this was how it *had* to be.

God understands all about walls, too: those strong, high enclosures we surround ourselves with, construct around us, hide within. We perceive them as our only way of protection and safety. Walls really can be a good thing - as long as there are doors and windows in them. This, unfortunately, is something we wall-builders often refuse to allow! For while not having doors may keep the "bad" out, having doors provides us with a way to allow the good to come in. While not having windows may keep us from being seen, having them provides a way for us to see out. It works both ways - something which those of us who lean toward "black-or-white thinking" often miss.

Diann describes some of her own experiences with walls. Perhaps you can relate:

Walls, walls, everywhere! That was one of the earliest discoveries I made when I first began this healing journey. It seemed as if everywhere I turned, there was another wall that needed to come down.

The Walls of Secrecy

"For there is nothing covered that will not be revealed, nor hidden that will not be known" (Luke 12:2 NKJ).

The very first wall I encountered was the wall of secrecy. The veil of silence and secrecy is a required part of an abuse victim's wardrobe. The "don't talk" rule is carved into the very soul of every abused child, whether that rule is clearly spoken or only understood to be a requirement, it is a rule that is seldom broken by the frightened child.

I had carried the secret of my sexual abuse for decades. The only person I had ever talked to about my father's inappropriate behavior was my mother. No one else either inside or outside the family was told until after I had become engaged to be married. I told my fiancé so that he could run if he wanted to do that. He chose not to run then and he has not run since. He has been a solid and stable rock in my life. Of course, when I told him about the abuse, I told him all that I knew about it at that time. I had not yet realized that the majority of the abuse was buried inside my subconscious mind. Telling him what I knew about it was the first feeble kick against the wall of secrecy.

Following my marriage, my new husband and I moved to another state that was nearly 1000 miles away from my childhood home and family members. I soon became close friends with Barbara, who proved to be a very caring and compassionate friend. She was the next person I told about my past. It felt like I was doing something very wrong at first by telling the family secret, but I soon discovered that telling the secret brought a sense of comfort to my soul; someone actually cared about me. Keeping the secret had caused me to be so numb in my emotions that I had never really felt much of anything. After sharing my secret with a compassionate friend, I felt validated and cared for. This brought a new freedom to my soul and over the years that followed, I shared my secret with two other people. This brought the number to a grand total of five people who knew about my sexually abusive past. I had gently begun to kick against the wall of secrecy, but I had made only a very small dent up to that point.

In 1997, our home church offered a sexual abuse recovery program. I was 51 years old at the time. I attended a weekend retreat that jump-started the recovery process and then I went through a 16-week group session in our church. The wall of secrecy had suffered a terrible blow this time. Following the group session, my pastor asked me if I would share my testimony with the church in a Sunday night service. I thought about it for a while and then agreed to do it, knowing that it would cost me in terms of family relationships. After sharing my testimony openly before our large church family, a deathblow was dealt to that wall of secrecy. The final blow to the wall came when I talked openly to my brothers about the abuse. Not one of my four brothers knew what happened to me until that time. From that day until now, I have had no trouble talking about my sexually abusive past. By sharing my story, I know that God will use it to bring hope and healing into many other wounded hearts and lives.

My Dirty Laundry
by Lexy

I'm burning my sheets -
they still feel dirty
even after all these months.
Your breath has seeped in
to my sheets and my brain.
I hear you laughing
every time my life
takes a turn for the worst.
I feel your touch

Kicking the Walls

> *sultry and sweat-damp*
> *in the middle of the night*
> *to startle me out of sleep.*
> *I walk quietly*
> *so I don't disturb you*
> *even though you aren't here*
> *and haven't been here*
> *for some time.*
> *Your breath,*
> *your words,*
> *your scorn,*
> *cling to the walls like mildew*
> *and infiltrate my sheets*
> *and my dreams*
> *and my peace.*
> *I'm burning my sheets,*
> *the flames lick up in tongues,*
> *telling the harsh truth:*
> *you are burned into my soul*
> *a canker I can't cut out*
> *a shadow on every thought*
> *a smirk on every triumph.*

Afterward
by Lexy:

When I look back on these words I wrote, I feel like crying. I don't want to cry so much for myself, but for all the others who still live behind the wall of secrecy. After years of floundering in secular counseling, I finally found a loving, understanding, Godly woman who helped guide me through the enemy's lies to a new life. The walls have been crushed to dust. I don't have to hide in shame and secrecy. My life is a beautiful and whole experience. The thoughts, which used to dominate me - the shame and worthlessness with which I was raised and bound - have been replaced by the knowledge that God made me, and He did not make garbage. I am fearfully and wonderfully made! Still, I cry for those who still live boxed in by the walls. It is hard to topple them down, but it is worth it. I never imagined life could be like this.

Walls of Denial

And I said to my heart, Shut be thy door to pain!

Denial can be one of the most difficult barriers to healing. When we have been trained to deny our pain, to deny our need, we find that getting the necessary help in order for healing to occur will be nearly impossible.

We were created with needs - needs for fellowship, intimacy, purpose, usefulness, dignity, love, companionship, safety. Somehow, though, somewhere along the line, we came to believe that having need was bad, was proof of our weakness, which somehow lessened our worth and robbed us of our dignity.

Unmet needs, however, will leave us desperate for some kind of relief, fast! We will literally be driven by what we *perceive* we need, even if it is to be thought of as "together" and "having everything under control" in our lives. Sadly, denial leaves us in the dark, so to speak, about what our true needs even are. Whether we admit them or not, though, our internal sense of unmet neediness, whether we admit to it or not, will leave us vulnerable and unprotected, even while we are in the process of vehemently denying that we have any need at all. It is simply not possible to have our needs taken care of while simultaneously denying them.

What causes such ambivalence in our feelings of having need <u>and</u> having the need to deny them all at once? *It can often be traced to the well-fortified walls of denial surrounding us.*

Denial is the saddest form of deception, and often is the very thing that allows evil to prevail. We deceive ourselves when we tell ourselves (and others) that we have need of nothing and no one, when we refuse to allow the very help that God would provide for us so that our needs can be met. Unfortunately, it takes a strong sense of our own personal identity to have the internal fortitude to admit to having needs, especially when our families and communities have taught us that this is clearly unacceptable. What we believe about ourselves and having those needs will be the determining factor in not only how those needs will be met but also whether we will allow them to be met at all.

For the abuse survivor, admitting to the pain and damage that occurred would force us to have to face that pain, along with the deep need for help, support, comfort, and healing. That would lead to needing people who would come alongside us in that process. That would require vulnerability, trust, hope - things we have invested deeply in not needing.

For many of us, denial serves another purpose; denial keeps us in a state of indecision. Somehow we think that if we just put off the decisions necessary for change to occur that we will be protected from the potential consequences of making bad ones. We hope that change for the better will happen without any pain or effort on our part. All too often, unfortunately, all we accomplish is putting off the inevitable.

In this next excerpt from a short story by Robyn we see this very issue addressed:

Love On The Rocks

> How many things have been taken away, never to return? Like jewels stolen in the night, innocence is lost. How many losses do I have, how many can I grieve, how many more are hidden in deep dark recesses of my mind? Dark, like a landmine dormant minefield in old war zones, still killing and maiming random victims a lifetime later, it lies. Closing my eyes I can pan across the last twenty-five years of my life and

see most of it, though not all. Some things are too painful to remember while others are so painful I wish I could forget.

My divorce has been final for six months; our separation turns five on Memorial Day. Still I mourn the marriage that I held onto so tenaciously, like a dog with a favorite sock toy. It is the same union that Bill thought would last forever, even if he never worked at saving it. I tried to give him what he wanted, I always made concessions for him, never held him responsible when he should have been, never threw his shortcomings in his face. Well, hardly ever.

I think back on nights I would curl next to his back, holding him from behind, a human life preserver trying to save him from drowning in his alcoholism. Me and "Bud," always at odds with each other and pulling from opposite ends of reality, mine stark and hard, "Bud's" soft and slurry. I guess it's no surprise that Bud won the tug of war. Perhaps I gave up too soon, but then I think of twenty years of trying, and hope that I just waited too long to admit the inevitable.

I would sleep with him in my arms, praying and loving him. Knowing that he was a sick man, one that needed help. He was too proud to ask for it, saying, "I got myself here and I'll get myself out." Well, he was wrong. He's still there and I'm not. I've dedicated myself to building a new life that is functional and real and sober. I've given myself over to the rhetoric of twelve step programs and listening to others who need to talk, who need to lance the boil of addiction and hatred, and let the putrid truth out in an atmosphere that is safe. Men and women alike, who are still trying to stick it out, trying to understand the maze of denial they have lived in for so many years of their lives, and how they got there…

How do we "get there?" Finding the answer to that question is often the very key that unlocks the door that leads to the way out. *That's the value of the process. That's also why it's worth breaking down the walls that hinder it.*

Kicking the Walls

For too many of us, looking for ways to protect ourselves from the fearful and unknown world around us comes so naturally we often miss the problem it is causing us. There are numerous ways and means that we resort to in order find at least some perceived protection for all the things around us that we cannot control. Self-protective means will be employed in ways we aren't aware of. It's all about what we believe about our world and the people who inhabit it. How does one keep safe in such an unpredictable environment?

The next wall we want to discuss here is written by Diann, and the artwork was drawn by Angie.

By Angie

The Walls of Self-Protection
By Diann

"He shall cover thee with His feathers, and under His wings shalt thou trust; His Truth shall be thy shield and buckler" (Ps. 91:4 KJV).

Protecting myself had become a way of life. The misuse and abuse I had encountered early in life taught me to keep up my guard at all times. It made perfect sense to me; if even my own parents failed to provide the necessary protection from harm, then I would simply take care of myself. Year after year, the thick walls of self-protection continued to be reinforced. The home I came from taught me over and over again to take care of myself. I can still hear my mother's words of warning: "If you don't take care of yourself, no else will." That tape played over and over in my mind. As a result of the abuse and those words of warning, I built walls around my wounded soul. No one would ever be allowed to get close enough to hurt me like that again. I would see to it, I would take care of myself. I lived for decades under those subconscious thoughts. Many people who entered my life found they could go only so far, and then they would run into that terrible wall. That protective wall which was designed to keep others away, had actually imprisoned me.

The weekend I attended the abuse recovery retreat, God showed me my protective apparel. The dress I had chosen to wear was a shroud; I had become the walking dead. The convicting power of the Holy Spirit melted my heart that afternoon as I repented of my sin of self-protection. This wall of self-protection had to come down and repentance was the wrecking ball that broke through to freedom.

I wish I could say that allowing God to be my Protector happened quickly and easily in that moment. It didn't happen either quickly or easily, in fact, I still struggle from time to time with bouts of self-protection. The old tape had to be erased and a new one written.

Kicking the Walls

I have found that God is faithful and that He will, according to Psalm 91, give His angels charge over me. The key is learning to dwell in the secret place of the Most High. I am learning that when I want to run, the best place to run to is that secret place of the Most High God. He will tenderly hide us under His wing and shelter us from harm.

There are other walls, too. Emotional walls, spiritual walls, and all the things that drive us, press on us, to keep them carefully reinforced should any crack dare to show…

Walls of Frustration

When we begin to recognize that we need to be on the other side of the walls.

Everyone experiences frustration from time to time, but when frustration begins to drive and control us it is a sure sign that something is very wrong. Perpetual feelings of frustration often come from our own deep sense of powerlessness over our circumstances, proof of our lack of control. Until we come to a brand new resolution from within us that "being in control" (which we NEVER really are anyway!) is not the only way to safety we will never experience the peace that God desires for us to have.

Diann writes:
Frustrated?
Who me?
Oh sure, there have been times when I wanted to kick something
Or throw something
Or just yell and scream into the wind.
Why can't people understand my pain?
Why can't they understand that I need them to just be there for me.
Why does everyone always say "just put it behind you and get on with the rest of your life"?
Don't they know I'd like nothing more than to get on with my life?
But, right now, recovery is my life.
I can't have a life until I do this.

I know it is taking longer than anyone thinks it should.
It is taking longer than I thought it would.
But, I didn't get here overnight and I'm sure I won't get this mess untangled overnight.
Isn't it enough to battle for truth and wholeness without having to battle for
My place in the family
My place in church
My place in this world
Why does everything have to be such a struggle?
And why do you have to put labels on me?
I have a name.
I'm a person.
Not a disorder.
My life is in disorder.
My mind is in disorder.
But, I'm still a person.
I have feelings.
Frustrated? Me?
Yes. Me.
I'm frustrated!

Walls of Self-Determination

"I will do it myself! I don't need any thing or any body.
I will not allow myself to be weak or needy. No matter what they put before me, I will not cry, seek, or ask for help. I will not complain.
And I will not tell what it's really like inside!"

Sound familiar? You know how it goes…

Diann writes this:

> *Grit. Determination. Pull yourself up by your own bootstraps.*
> These were the qualities of value and worth within my family.
> Do it yourself.

Kicking the Walls

Take pride in doing it alone, never needing anyone or anything.
Suck it up and keep going.

That's why it has been so hard for me to be open and allow others to come alongside me in this journey. Needing help was a sign of weakness.
I didn't want to be weak.
Look what being weak brought into my life…
No. I would never be weak and needy again.
But inside this hidden inner part of me, I am weak and I am needy.
I cry inside where no one can see or hear.
I cry because I am so very needy.

God knows how weak I truly am.
He promised that He would be strong in my weakness.
But promises have been made before.

So, I muster all the determination I have and I press on.
Inside, I still cry.
Inside, I am weak.
Inside, I need you.
But I press on…alone.

What we often do in situations that require us to behave as if there is no excuse for not performing, for not carrying out the instructions given us is, as one survivors puts it, "just suck it up." The message comes through loud and clear that who we are or how abuse affects us is inconsequential to those who could and should stop it but choose not to. So we draw upon our own resources, or if necessary, we create them. This poem by C.T. expresses just such an internal process.

Just Before Dawn

Carry On!

*Carry on! they tell me,
however hard it seems.
Push on and up and forward
by all and every means.
No weakness, now, nor faltering
will we from you allow!
We care not what it costs you
nor what you feel, nor how.
We demand full compliance,
and nothing less will do,
it matters not, your weeping,
for we care not for you.
So stop this silly whining
and falling on old traits,
and hurry to the tasks at hand,
they simply cannot wait!
Just carry on, they tell me,
no concern of ours the price,
nothing less than more than all
will our demands suffice.
You know by now the system
and how to work within,
there's no relief or freedom (from it),
you simply cannot win.
So stop your vain lamenting
and counting up your woe,
and stop your fool excusing,
Get off your self and go!*

As people seeking to heal from abuse, we often find that we need to make major shifts in our thinking when it comes to accepting help, comfort, sympathy, or having needs. Since these things were simply not allowed when we were in our abusive situations, it is difficult, to say the least, to retrain ourselves to think that longing for help and support and comfort when it is appropriate should indeed be allowed.

Kicking the Walls

This next essay by Niid la'i is a powerful example of how many of us were taught that "needing" was something that was absolutely not allowed, not to be expected or voiced, or even recognized. A note here: Niid la'i is a survivor of Satanic Ritual abuse. Her reference to "alters" refers to what psychologists refer to as dissociative states, discussed in other sections of this book. While this particular form of abuse is certainly less prevalent (and most certainly less talked about), the effects of any type of abuse is something all survivors can relate to.

On Having Need

This is an essay on need. Need is frightening to me. I don't want to have need! The voices of programming inside start to shout at me when I acknowledge that I have needs. I am not supposed to have needs. I have always existed to serve others. I am supposed to be compliant, understanding, and forgiving, no matter what anyone does to me, or says to me. I am never supposed to express an opinion, or discontent or dissatisfaction.

As a child, I learned to have a "nothing face." This face was devoid of all expression. It was a face that hid a million feelings. Sometimes, even this expression was unacceptable.
If it was misconstrued as sullen, then punishment descended on me anyway. I had to have at least a suggestion of a smile and contentment blended in with the nothing face. It was used when cult members were present and in the home with the mother and father.

I also have what I call "outside faces." Outside faces are more readable. They were created to present a pleasant, calm, and amiable appearance to all people. The outside faces went to school and to relatives' homes and to public places. As a small child, people would comment on how quiet I was. As a teenager, and even now, many friends and acquaintances tell me I am so "laid back!" What a joke! But it proves how well everyone inside has hidden behind the acceptable faces that afforded some safety.

One problem this has created is a numbing affect. In order for the outside faces and the nothing face to function, needs and feelings had to be literally forgotten. If alters, which I call, "others," inside were too upset or anxious, there was a possibility of their emotions breaking through. Often in a cult gathering, members of the group would convince little others that if they had feelings inside, the members could tell. So, even if their facial expression were as it should be, the cult members would punish them for the feelings these "little people", my name for little alters, were supposedly having. Because of this, others learned to deny their feelings and more others were created to hold feelings in far away worlds. Their needs were not recognized anymore either. Eventually they were as "nothing" inside as their faces learned to be on the outside.

When one of my alters was 6 years old she was being taught not to cry. I'm sure there were lots of other "lessons" already ingrained about showing emotions, but this is just one description of those indoctrination sessions. The memory, and I'm sure it is not complete, is of this small child standing naked in front of a male adult. He was sitting in a chair and all of a sudden he slapped her very hard on the cheek. Of course, she grabbed her cheek and started to cry. He removed her hand and hit her again and said simply, "Don't cry!" She tried to stop but couldn't. He continued to hit her cheek and repeat the words until her tears stopped and the only evidence of the pain was her labored breathing. I'm sure that at some point this little person inside fragmented into others who could hold the sting of the slaps and even the tears away from her six-year old consciousness. Eventually, she was able to stand dry eyed in front of her abuser and not even flinch. By the time this was accomplished, her cheek and eye were so swollen and bruised that she could not go to school for more than a week.

Kicking the Walls

Certainly, everyone who lives on the earth has the need to cry many times in his/her life. But for me, because of countless, repeated episodes of controlled programming such as the one just described, my need to cry was effectively shut off. Now, as an adult, though I need to cry, there are many times I can't.
I will feel tears begin to fill my eyes and my throat tighten up, but then all the symptoms just go away. I am left with an overwhelming sadness, a stomachache and extreme anxiety.

Can I then tell anyone I am anxious, or sad, or feel sick? NO! Others inside have been taught equally well that they are not supposed to ask for relief or comfort. They should not even feel sad, or anxious or sick. If they do have these feelings, they think they are bad and evil for having them. They experience tremendous guilt and shame.

In the present day, I find I don't understand what is happening with my emotions. I go to the Dr. and get so anxious when I have to tell him/her what is wrong that I get tongue-tied and confused. The Dr. gets impatient and frustrated because my explanations are so disjointed. He/she misunderstands. I try again, but I still can't be clear. I am then judged incompetent and a hypochondriac. I am treated with lack of respect and in a mocking way. I don't understand why I can't talk to doctors.
I feel stupid and ashamed for being so evasive and indirect.

This happens because I am not supposed to need. If I am sick, I am not supposed to need help. I am not supposed to tell anyone I don't feel good. I am not supposed to GET sick in the first place. This is ludicrous when considered logically. Everyone gets sick. But, the lessons are still so much a part of me, I think I am bad and evil for wanting medicine to feel better.

Let's say I go to a therapy session. I am going to therapy because I am trying to resolve the conflicts I sense inside. Even being there is a serious breach of "the rules." Again, I am admitting I have needs, and I am trying to talk to someone about them. Talking is akin to murder. It is a capital offense and carries major consequences if broken. Therapy is all about talking! If I sit silent in front of my therapist then nothing is accomplished. If I speak to him I am buried in angry, shouting inner voices, pleading voices, scared voices. My body starts to hurt in various places. I cannot think again, and what I say comes out jumbled and incoherent. I get frustrated and panic-stricken. If my therapist shows even the slightest indication of impatience or perceived anger, everyone inside withdraws. All the others inside willing to watch and listen are so hyper alert they notice every movement, twitch and voice inflection the therapist has. This can seriously impede progress in therapy.

Many times I have left a session thinking the therapist has labeled me needy and draining. This is because if I ask him/her for anything: reassurance, understanding, support, I think I am being overbearing and demanding. The very act of walking through the door of the office and being seen feels like asking for more than anyone should ever be asked to give. Indeed, I am supposed to go in there and figure out what the therapist needs and start supporting and taking care of him! Paradoxically, if the therapist cannot return a rare phone call, or cannot be as supportive as I need him/her to be, I feel rejected and abandoned. So, I find myself in one of those double binds so common to survivors. If the therapist is supportive, I feel bad and evil. If he is not supportive, I feel bad and evil. This is all because I am not supposed to have any needs.

What can happen is that I get so worried about being needy that I become needy! By skirting around what I really want to say or ask for, those who are working with me have to guess at what I am really trying to ask or say. They can end up feeling manipulated or like they are being forced to play some strange kind of game. Though this is not my intent, especially if they do not know me very well, my "half-talk," as I call it, can create the very drain I am trying so hard not to inflict on others.

It's another trust issue. In order to heal, I have to trust. But before I can trust I need to be able to learn to trust! I have to risk from the very foundation of my being. I wear the lessons of the past like a second skin. To begin removing this skin leaves me feeling touch tender and naked once again. I often feel like I am metaphorically standing in the middle of a busy freeway daring the cars not to hit me. That's how vulnerable I feel as I try and shed the beliefs that have ruled me from the day I was born. I hate it when I am told I am comfortable living within the boundaries placed on me from the past. But, it is true. I have only known what I was so methodically programmed to believe.

Learning new ways is filled with as much pain and anxiety as the original abuse. As I discover and then acknowledge that I have needs and attempt to trust these needs to "outsiders," "big people," i.e., therapists, doctors and friends, I open myself up to the possibility of more hurt and misunderstanding. Though these people are not abusers, human beings are subject to making mistakes, responding from their own set of rules. The everyday problems in relationships that are bound to happen when people get together can seem as intense as the former abuse.

Can the voices of programming ever be silenced? I hope so. At this point, I have to rely on my therapists and other caregivers to instruct me and guide me. I cannot offer concrete ways to implant trust in barren soil. What this essay offers is insight.
I NEED those who read it to understand and be able to step beyond my walls of resistance and help me. I hope that as other survivors relate to these barriers that affect their healing they will also seek out people that can assist them to shed their old skins of the past. Now how's this for breaking programming!

Walls of Self-Contempt

It's strange, when you really think about it, that the ones who have been so wounded and cruelly used by the wrongful, selfish choices of others would be so quick - even willing - to place the blame and hate on themselves for what was perpetrated against them.

Yet we do that. Perhaps that's the only thing we *can* control during the abuse, or after it. As Ann explains, "If I am the problem, I can fix it myself by self contempt and self punishment. I can't bear the helplessness of being a victim with no recourse, nor the realization that someone I love is evil and does not love me." Either way, it is certainly the safest route. "If I look closely enough," another survivor writes, "I will always find that I am most certainly the safest person to be mad at: I don't hit back. I am the very best at being my own worst enemy." After all, the reasoning goes, bad things happen to bad people, right? This seems to makes sense, to fit our natural sense of justice, at least it does to a child with an unformed concept of self. These next few poems paint a picture from a child's point of view something about what this is like.

Ribbons of Gold and Red
By Diann

I came to you wrapped up in pretty ribbons of gold and red
You took a look at my tiny package and just shook your head
My ribbons sparkled with light as they curled about in haphazard array
"No, these curly unruly ribbons are too messy, this is how they should lay."

You pulled and tugged and worked and planned out all my ways.
You plotted, planned and fashioned for me all my days.
The curly, sparkly brightly shining ribbons in your hand then limply lay

Kicking the Walls

> Til my red faded into pastel pink, my gold became a deathly shade of gray.
>
> Within your controlling grasp as you labored all the more
> You struggled with the freedom that my aching soul yearned for
> To break away from fingers always seeking to re-form my very form;
> Till the day arrived when your faded ribboned package simply could not bear your scorn.
>
> Now Someone else has placed His hands upon my strings of life
> His touch frees my very soul from stifling, suffocating strife.
> He restores my ribbons red and gold their sparkle and their light
> He hides me from the darkness as He breathes with my soul, His Breath of Life.

Abuse does more than ravage the body of those who experience it, it tears at our very souls and severs us from our hearts and minds. What is left in its wake is a loss too great to express in words. It affects absolutely everything - our sense of who we are as people, our future hope and expectation, our sense of worth as human beings. Jamie writes about it this way:

Jamie's Self-Worth

> Your questing fingers
> Sculpted my sand castle
> And then destroyed it
> My self worth was never what it should have been
>
> Gabriel and Michael ascend to the Milky Way
> Symphony left me alone and old
> The 3 Musketeers turned their backs on me

Just Before Dawn

Their Snickers of laughter
Amplified my loss of hope

They threw me a solo Rolo
I picked it up
With heaven in my eyes
El Dorado was discovered in my heart

Clark Bar came along and took my solo Rolo
And replaced it with a single M&M
I began to cry
He says to me
"It could be worse, you could have no candy
Be thankful you are worth a single M&M."

My self worth was in place.

Self-hate is another common by-product of abuse. This may be a difficult concept to understand for many people, but thinking about it from a child's point of view, it does make sense. If bad things are happening, things too terrible to even talk about, things that other people find shameful and disgusting, what other conclusions can the victim come to? The perpetrators most certainly do not explain that the horrible things happening are *their* fault and responsibility!

Self-Hate
(Author unknown)

Why do we hate ourselves, but love that which created us?
When I gaze
Into my own eyes
I see not beauty
Not strength
Not love

A stamp of self hate
In dripping, bold, red ink

Kicking the Walls

> *Brazing my forehead*
> *"Void"*
>
> *When I gaze*
> *into Your eyes*
> *I see love*
> *Compassion*
> *Divinity*
>
> *Why*
> *When we see ourselves*
> *Do we dispraise what*
> *Has been passed onto us*
> *By such a gentle*
> *Kind and gracious touch?*

Walls of Despair

> *"I hated life...So my heart began to despair..." (Ecc. 2:20).*
> *"O my soul, why art thou disquieted within me?" (Ps. 43:5).*

When depression and despair sink their cruel claws into us for the long stay, life can become toilsome indeed. Despair is one of the highest, thickest walls to break through. Often before we realize it, we've built ourselves into a prison from which there seems to be no escape, ever. It is during these times that we are in grievous danger, for hope deferred makes more than just the heartsick. We lose our objectivity, and our capacity to tolerate the things happening around us lessens as we become more and more depleted. Like the shadow of a small object becomes magnified and takes on some other appearance, so despair casts its shadow upon our souls and distorts our view.

I mourn,
I cry,
I kick the wall,
and plead for some relief.

Just Before Dawn

None comes.
Now what?
I've no one to turn to, no one to listen, no one to help me.
I'm alone.
And everything within me sinks down, waiting to die, and hoping it will be soon.
This is what despair is like.
This is me.

Where, then, is hope to be found? Where is the dawn's light that will bring warmth to the cold nighttime of our souls? When despair threatens to overwhelm us completely, where does the wherewithal come from in order that we might continue on and see the journey's end? Perhaps it begins right here, now, in this place that we are, whatever it looks like. First, we must recognize it, give it a name. Leigh called it "an empty void."

> *There is an empty void*
> *That causes ceaseless pain*
> *No human song can ease the hurt*
> *Nor heartless faces numb the ache*
>
> *No work or play distract the mind*
> *From loneliness*
>
> *No tears can help*
> *Nor self-pity heal the wound*
> *That eats away the soul*

Until we are able to find the source of that kind of despair, it seems impossible to escape its icy grasp upon us.

> *In dark despair there works a villain*
> *Boring into the heart of man*
> *To make his suffering deep*
> *He whispers thoughts of sorrow*
> *And sucks his victims down into*
> *A swirling mire of bitterness*

Kicking the Walls

> *Deeper and deeper sinks the wretched soul*
> *He sees no escape*
> *Only blinding despondence*
> *No hope...no hope...*

But the story does not end here! As we seek God and accept His help we will begin to be able to see from a new perspective, and to find that escape we so desperately need.

> *Open your blinded eyes*
> *And see the glorious Light*
> *Let Him pull you out of your bitter mire!*
> *And cleanse you with His blood*
> *For He is a friend of the friendless*
> *A Light in the darkness of despair*
> *He is Eternal*
> *Help*
> *And Hope*
> *And Victory!*

At one especially low point in her healing process one survivor asked God her hard questions. She faced her innermost heart's pain and fear, and what came to her as she prayed was this song:

Trusting Abba
By MaryAnn

Can He see the well of hurt hidden within me?
Little girl, can't face the world, does He hear my plea?

Longin' to cry out to Him, but oh I'm so afraid
That like the rest, He'll try His best, but turn the other way.

I want to trust, yes, feel I must, accept His Father hand,
But somehow can't believe or grant that He will understand.

Just Before Dawn

*Beloved child, I won't defile
My character is sure.
Can't you see, there could not be
A love more right or pure?
Abba "Daddy," trust My Name.
Others failed, I'm not to blame.
Do not be afraid to call
Abba Father, Lord of all.*

What I've believed was fantasy, not really true at all.
My broken heart, the child-like part, resists His loving call.

Can love exist, without a twist, no aftermath of shame?
Can there be a certainty that His love's not the same?

If trust's betrayed, mistakes been made, how do I begin
To lay aside the fear I hide, at letting Him come in?

*Beloved child, I won't defile
My character is sure.
Can't you see, there could not be
A love more right or pure?*

*Abba "Daddy," trust My Name.
Others failed, I'm not the same.
Do not be afraid to call
Abba Father, Lord of all*

Pretence leaves, my spirit grieves for what love should have been.
Now I'm bereft at what is left. Will I be hurt again?

Can Abba prove that He will move mountains for my cause?
In every way, can He display a Father without flaws?

85

Could it be, He waits for me to simply realize,
Trust will unfold as I behold the love His cross implies.

Beloved child, I won't defile
My character is sure.
Can't you see, there could not be
A love more right or pure?

Abba "Daddy," trust My Name.
Others failed, I'll heal your pain.
Do not be afraid to call
Abba Father, Lord of all.

My Own Personal Wailing Wall
By Diann

Here I am again…with my nose pressed up against this wall. I am tired and drained. I don't want to do this anymore. I'm sick of this process. I'm tired of trying and tired of crying. Yet, here I am one more time. Curled up in a ball on the sofa with my face pressed deeply into the rough texture of the fabric. I can moan and groan into the back of the sofa, allowing it to absorb the cries of my anguished soul. I can cry tears of anger and frustration, allowing the sage green Wailing Wall to absorb my tears.

What's the point of this anyway? I'm too old for this! It happened too long ago. What does it matter now anyway? Even my own internal 'parts' are old…they've been with me more than 50 years. My 'kids' are 50 years old! I spent 20 years living in abuse and now I've invested five more years in trying to become whole. I'm not sure I will ever make it anyway…not sure there are enough years left to do this…maybe I'm just too old. I know I'm too tired. I just want to quit. I don't want to do this anymore. And so I wail and wail into the wall…while God patiently allows me to vent my anger and frustration with the process and with myself and yes, with even Him.

Just Before Dawn

Sometimes this seems like some kind of sadistic joke. God, why did you wait until I became an 'old' woman before you touched my wounds? I'm not young anymore. I'm well into my 50's. Why now? Why not 20 years ago? It would have made so much more sense to me twenty years ago.

And so I wail some more into my sage green Wailing Wall. Answers don't come, but the tears do.

After five years, what has been accomplished?

I am more in touch with my own feelings…I've even learned that it's okay to be angry sometimes.

I'm no longer a 'people pleaser.' I am a God pleaser.

I learned that "keeping the peace at any cost" isn't really a good idea. When the cost is denying the cries of my own soul, then the cost is too great. I matter too.

I learned when and how to say "No!"
I learned that 'pretending' to be okay isn't okay.

I learned that trying to carry other people's baggage isn't required. I have enough of my own without carrying some else's.

I learned to cast my cares. God is ready, willing and able to carry my problems, just as He carries me.

I learned that life is full of disappointments. Being disappointed won't kill me; its just part of life.

I've learned how to be more 'open' with others. Maybe I'm not quite where I should be yet on this one, but I'm not where I used to be either.

I learned that God wants us to know the truth, even when the truth is painful. Living and believing a lie is an affront to Him. He is Truth and there is no lie in Him. Denial believes a lie, or at best, only a half-truth.

I learned that a lot of people in this world really do care about me.

I learned that I care about people and I have something worthwhile to pour into a lot of their lives.

I learned that there is nothing wrong with the way I think or speak.
I am a unique individual, created by God. There is no one else quite like me! Thank God!

I learned that God understands me even when I don't.

I learned that God is ahead of me, behind me and right alongside me all the time.
He is also 'For' me.

I am able to be more comfortable in social settings than I was five years ago. Again, I'm not where I'd like to be, but I'm better.

I learned that sometimes just surviving is good enough. I learned that being able to endure qualifies as being of strong faith. I'm still here.

I learned that God loves me!
I learned that God loves me too much to leave me where I am.

Walls of Fear

"Fear not..."

It was surprising to me when I actually realized how often the Word talks about fear. The many *'fear-nots'* don't bring condemnation to me anymore, but rather help me to thankfully realize that God knows what a huge issue this can be for His people. Life is full of legitimate things to be concerned about, things and people and situations that produce anxiety and distress for all of us at some time or another.

Just Before Dawn

Fear and its accompanying feelings are real, whether our fears are justified or not.

As survivors of abuse, we are often subject to fears that many people cannot begin to understand. "What's the big deal about? It's *just* a nightmare!" (Or flashback, or trigger, or threat, or lie, or belief, or whatever.) "Why can't you just forget it and move on? All that stuff happened a long time ago - *Get over it!"* Whatever one's intention for trying to "set the survivor straight," when this occurs it often serves to set back the healing process and makes getting past the resulting issues of abuse even more difficult. The Word of God is full of examples of open lament! Where, then, have we come to the conclusion that getting over it is a spiritual principle? It's difficult to imagine Job not mourning for his children, or Tamar just getting over being raped by her own brother. Those lives were forever affected in some way by their past experiences.

To add to the pain of all those things our past experiences have caused us to be so sensitive to, we are hyper-vigilant and watchful of any hint of disapproval or scorn in the eyes of others. We have the fear of being misunderstood, of being unjustly accused, of our powerlessness and lack of control, of being taken advantage of, of being labeled as overly sensitive, hysterical, melodramatic...The list goes on.

One survivor put it this way:

> *Sometimes it's hard for me to feel comfortable around other people because they have NO clue about the horrors of my past, and if they ever did find out, I'd be shunned, to say the least.*

Is this an unjustified fear on her part? Taking into account similar reports from hundreds of other survivors, the answer is: absolutely not! It is not an issue of people, for the most part, intentionally being mean spirited or insensitive, but that many of us cannot relate to or tolerate those issues in our own lives that we have not dealt with ourselves, for whatever reason. Our pain makes people uncomfortable, ill at ease, or feeling overwhelmed. They simply do

Kicking the Walls

not have the resources to deal with it. Unfortunately, we can suffer "secondary abuse" as a result. And so the walls remain intact. Diann shares her thoughts on fear:

> I don't believe it is possible for anyone to go through abuse of any kind without experiencing fear. Fear is a God-given natural emotion. We learn to fear things that can bring harm to us. As a small child, we learn not to place our hand on a hot stove burner; touching the hot burner will cause us to fear to touch it again. However, if we go through life always being afraid of stove burners, we will never be able to cook our food. Healthy fear is one thing, but unhealthy fear is an extremely crippling emotion. Unhealthy fear binds us up in chains, holds us down, holds us back, and prevents us from being able to move forward, to grow and become the person that God created us to be. What losses are produced in our lives because of fear!
>
> I am able to look back now and see where I used to be. Thank God, I'm not there anymore; however, I still have battles with fear. God is gracious to me in this area. He tells me not to worry about the things I cannot do yet, just keep on doing the things I can and trust Him with the rest. There are still times when I want to run away and hide, and sometimes I do just that; however, God comes and gets behind the wall of fear and calls me to face it. The key to being free from fear is repentance. When I discover areas of my life where fear tries to control me, I repent of the fear and ask God to help me keep going. The repentance breaks the chains of fear and allows me to move forward once again. Fear is not God's plan for any life. Scripture has much to say regarding fear.
>
> *"There is no fear in love; but perfect love casts out fear, because fear involves torment, but he who fears has not been made perfect in love"*
> *(I John 4:18 NKJ).*

"Do not fear, for you will not be ashamed; neither be disgraced, for you will not be put to shame, for you will forget the shame of your youth..." (Isa. 54:4 NKJ).

Through His word, God has given us the tools we need to overcome fear.

Through repentance of fear's hindering power over our lives and through the renewing of our minds by meditating on His word, we are well able to tear down the walls of fear and to become victorious in life.

A Fearsome and Dreadful Thing Defeated

When will this fearsome dreadful thing find its end?
It too long has been my most dreadful friend.

The intertwining tendrils of my childhood past
In gray clouds of shame and fear were darkly cast.

The bands of fear and dread slowly lose their hold.
This dreadful friend who once seemed so strong and bold.

The cords of fear which once so strongly held me back,
Begin to break! And snap! And free me from their dreadful trap.

This dreadful friend I once thought would never leave,
Holds on now, as by a single thread; friendship bereaved.

Yes! Take your flight, you fearsome battled foe, defeated!
In the Presence of my Conquering King, remain I seated.

Kicking the Walls

Walls of Anger/Rage

"Doest thou well to be angry?" Jonah 4:4

The pent up emotions that come as a result of the pain, fear, injustice and powerlessness experienced by abuse survivors are incredibly intense. Perhaps that is why we are so afraid of them.

Mine is such a pretty wall
Pleasant all about
I keep my plastic mask in front
Allow no hint of doubt
But back behind the sweet façade
A fearful monster dwells
And if I once should slip and speak...
No! I must never tell!
That deep within this quiet one
Another monster hides
And if just once makes her escape
All in her reach would die

Most of us don't know how to be angry. At least, not appropriately. When pain and fear combine, the mix can be toxic. The poison of buried rage insidiously spreads throughout our being, often presenting itself in ways that keep us unaware of its presence. Because overt displays of anger were not allowed by our perpetrators we often found creative ways of stifling it, but those methods we used then cannot be expected to last. Invariably, they will find an outlet, somehow, some way. "I'm not angry," one survivor asserts, "it all happened so long ago. I just don't let it bother me. In fact, I hardly ever even think about it." What she also does not "think about" (at least in connection to her abuse) are her seemingly inexplicable bursts of anger, constant exhaustion, migraines, abdominal upsets, and the myriad of other unexplained physical and emotional cues her body and mind send her.

Anger and rage are terrifying to those who have been doubly hurt for displaying such emotions. "I'm afraid that if I let my anger out it will destroy everything I come into contact with!" This is a common fear of so many, often because we have seen the destructive power of rage as it was demonstrated by our perpetrators. What do we do with it then? For many, we aim it at the safest person around – ourselves. And we keep it well hidden, deep inside where no one can suspect it lurks. When asked to listen to the internal dialog inside for just a few moments, this is what one survivor heard:

> *This is really stupid and I don't want to do it. I'm afraid and I don't want to listen to the angry people that live inside my head. Well not my head, I think they are in my soul. I'm afraid that if I listen to them they will destroy me. That's really stupid because they are me. But they are a part of me I don't like to look at because they are bad, and that means I am bad. They are hungry, no, ravenous, looking for something to devour, and that would be me. I feel so little and scared! I want to run and hide so they can't get me and this is really stupid. Stupid thing from a stupid girl, stupid and fat and ugly and useless garbage. I hate you – me! Go ahead and read a book or eat something or go be busy so you can't hear me, but I'm here all the time. Waiting for a quiet moment when your guard is down and there is no one to help you, and then you are mine! I can dig into your vulnerable places with my sharp stick of hate and wound you, hurt you, make you cry...because I know you hate to cry. People say they like you, but I know what it is really inside you. We know what you really are, and everyone would run screaming from you if they saw. I'm much bigger than you and I can do whatever I want to you, if you let me out!*

Unfortunately, for someone who has suffered abuse this is no uncommon way to feel. The internal rage festering inside those who have cause to be angry but believe they have no safe way to express it will erode one's internal defenses. Those who stuff their rage will agonize over such intense emotions boiling within them. The internal anguish and pain they feel but are too afraid to express will not simply evaporate with the rising of the sun. It must be dealt with safely and appropriately and in the context of understanding and knowledgeable help.

Kicking the Walls

Diann writes about some of the lessons she has learned about anger:

> I was one of those people who thought anger was a sin. This was not surprising, because I had grown up in a home where anger was expressed as rage, on almost a daily basis. It frightened me, and so I was determined to live my life in a cool, even-tempered manner. Nothing could provoke an outburst from me, and I thought that was healthy.
>
> Little did I know that a seething kettle of anger and resentment was bubbling deep within my heart, a toxic brew of ugly memories, secrecy, shame and fear. Not only was I not in touch with my own emotions, but also I wasn't even in touch with my own reality.
>
> This couldn't last forever, and as I began seeking help for the wounds of childhood sexual abuse, the lid came off that kettle and released steam that could not be held back. It was an energy that was churning and moving and edging itself to the surface of my life. It was taking over, and I was afraid to allow it out. I knew this was anger, at long last released, and I had seen too many times what can happen when rage controls people.
>
> So I prayed for God to help me, and what he showed me to do with my anger may surprise you. I already knew where this angry energy was coming from—the nightmare of being molested, raped and abused from early childhood. But how to safely let it out? I paced restlessly in my backyard, then picked up an empty flowerpot and threw it against the concrete patio. The sound of it breaking was very satisfying to me, so I picked up another and repeated the process. The problem was that I needed my flowerpots. One of my adult sons, an avid hunter, suggested that I buy a box of clay targets (about four dollars) and use them to vent my feelings. But how? I saw the answer leaning, silent and strong, against the wall of my garage.

Just Before Dawn

And so I named each of the targets for an offense by my father, and then crushed them with a single swing from the heavy sledgehammer. One by one, as the tears that had been so long closed up within my soul began to flow freely.

I broke almost an entire box of clay targets that day—and as I smashed them, I prayed for God to release me from the anger and bitterness of my own soul. I repented for allowing those feelings to reside deep within me for so long, and then a strange thing happened. I began to feel the stirrings of forgiveness, and I realized that I was no longer chained to my past. Those chains, like the targets, had snapped beneath the force of the sledgehammer and the Holy Spirit's response to my prayers.

The way out of anger is through the gate of forgiveness, and what lies beyond that gate is love. Not the wimpy, fuzzy love that says, "Use me," or, "Abuse me," but love that is bold and unafraid to reach out and touch things that might be considered unlovely, unlovable and untouchable. Only when God sets us free from the pain of our past and releases our souls from anger and resentment are we truly free to love.

I've heard many abuse survivors say they could never love their abuser(s). Unless they first know and receive God's love, that is probably true. We cannot give away what we do not have, and many survivors did not receive appropriate love from their parents. Their love tank is empty. Through the working of the Holy Spirit, we are enabled to love others; by ourselves, it is often impossible.

Sadly, the forgiveness I offered my father had meant little to him, for shortly after that, he chose to molest my four-year-old son. When in his late teens, my son agreed to go on one of the same type of retreats for sexual abuse recovery in which I had participated. He attended the retreat because of behavior patterns he was seeing in his own life.

The men's retreat was powerful and my son came home renewed in his heart and mind. He continued to participate in a men's recovery group offered by our home church. Not too long after he completed his group sessions, he began to have bits and pieces of spontaneous memories of his own abuse. Slowly he began to put the pieces together, much like putting together a jigsaw puzzle. We now know what happened to him and also the areas of my son's life that need healing. I told him that I knew he would hold me responsible for his abuse and that I hoped one day he could find it in his heart to forgive me. I apologized for my failure to protect him and for leaving him in a very vulnerable position with a known perpetrator. My husband and I gladly paid for the retreat that my son attended and we have continued to provide him with help and support in every way possible. He has had remarkable improvement in many areas of his life, although he still continues to struggle in some areas.

On December 25, 2000, my son gave me one of the greatest gifts anyone could ever give me. He called me into his room and in a very broken voice, told me that he forgave me for my failure to protect him. He told me that he knew it wasn't my fault and he sobbed out his forgiveness before me. It was one of the most tender and moving moments of my life. To sit beside my grown son and hold him in my arms, sobbing along with him, receiving the tender forgiveness that my heart had needed for so many years, was a healing balm to my own soul as well as his. This is how forgiveness should work. It is beautiful and it is healing.

It grieves me that forgiveness doesn't always work out as it did between my son and me. However, no matter what the result of our offering of forgiveness, we simply must keep on forgiving. There is no other way to have peace and joy in this life. We are not to seek revenge, but simply to leave that to the One who judges with righteous judgment. We are called to forgive as God also forgives us and leave everything else in His hands.

Is it easy to forgive those who have so blatantly violated us? No. But God helped me to realize that the debt my father owed me was one I could not collect—forgiveness leaves the judgment and payment collecting to God, who judges righteously.

Following the release of my anger, I began to have a love in my heart for my father and other family members. My emotions were no longer in neutral, and I was free to love and care for even those who had so grossly damaged me years before.

My journey to forgiveness began, as it must, with the realization that my anger had to be released. No one could go through what I did without being angry. Yet anger either corrodes or explodes, and that is why God has made a way out of it for us. A difficult way, to be sure. The very mention of the word "forgive" causes many abuse survivors to bristle. Forgiveness is a choice that we make, and it is not an easy one. It is a process, not a one-time event. It requires going back time and again and letting go of the pain and releasing the abuser. No one can restore my childhood, my innocence or my virginity. That debt cannot be paid, so I chose to release from it the abusers who tormented my life.

"For if you forgive men their trespasses, your heavenly Father will also forgive you. But if you do not forgive men their trespasses, neither will your Father forgive your trespasses" (Matthew 6:14-15).

Beyond anger, through the gates of forgiveness, lies the strong, bold love of God.

Kicking the Walls

The Walls of Shame

"Those who look to Him are radiant; their faces are never covered with shame"
(Ps. 34:5 NIV).

What an amazing, incredible contrast to what so many of us wrestle with inside! Is it honestly possible that the shame we live with, way down in the innermost core of our being, can be transformed into something entirely new and different just by looking at God? Perhaps that depends on what we see when we look up. Or if we look up at all. Often we are so bound up by shame that we fear to do just that. Only a few things in life are more powerful than shame, and for many of us it seems too embedded to ever be free from its vice like grip. Shame keeps us bound up in ways that little else can, and while some walls may acceptably be thought of as potentially toppled down, this wall is one we are careful to keep hidden behind. Why? John Bradshaw writes in *Healing the Shame That Binds You*,

> Shame is experienced as the all-pervasive sense that I am flawed and defective as a human being. (It) gives you a sense of worthlessness, a sense of failing and falling short as a human being. (It) is a rupture of the self with the self…and is so excruciating because it is the painful exposure of the believed failure of self to the self (10).

Is it any wonder we want to keep these walls intact? If we should venture to muster up the courage to wander out, though, and we perceive that others are confirming our already inflamed sense of shame, we will believe we have no other recourse but to pull back yet again and retreat to our hiding place behind the walls, terrified to look out for what we might see.

Sad Reflection

When I see me in your eyes what there must I behold?
Will they again reflect my shame and leave me dead and cold?

Just Before Dawn

*They but bespeak the very fear that I have always thought
And bring me back to face again that I have tried for naught.*

*When I see me in your eyes I never measure up
But once again I drink the dregs that fill the bitter cup.
Again your gaze directs me to the low place I belong
and there requires I not forget my all and many wrongs.*

*Perhaps one day these eyes of mine will lift their saddened gaze
and find reflected something new to clarify this haze
my pain and failure bring about. Perhaps one day I'll see
a look that says, You've done enough, now come, and rest, and be.
One that says, I will accept the person that you are,
one that looks beyond the many places I am marred,
that offers back acceptance that I cannot ever earn.
O Father God! Once again, to You alone I turn...*

                                            and hide my face.

Thankfully, God never stops there. He is in the redeeming business, the business or restoration and rebuilding. Scripture is full of such examples, revealing the heart of God in this matter. The hardest part is getting started, looking up, right into the eyes of Abba God, and allowing Him the opportunity to prove to us that He really is different, that He really will not look upon us in scorn and shame us yet again. It's taking a huge chance from our perspective. But then, that's what the healing process is all about. Ultimately, a complete restoration of fellowship and oneness with our God.

Walls of Unforgiveness

*Choosing to Forgive When We've Been Wounded
An article by Karenjoy*

Some years ago, I was invited to speak at a conference on healing. There were several speakers presenting workshops on various subjects. What was interesting about this particular conference was that the subjects were assigned to us. I have to admit that when I first opened up that announcement and saw the subject I would be speaking on (the announcements were already typed up and mailed out), my first reaction was not a real 'spiritual' one. *They want me to talk about what?? Forgiveness!?!* All I could think of was, *I can't do this! I'm not qualified! I don't think I really know enough about this!* But then God said to me, *"Tell them that they cannot teach or give away something they do not have for themselves."*

Of course, He was speaking directly to me. Needless to say, the following weeks were indeed an incredible challenge for me, but one I would not have missed out on (even if I could have), because every time we go God's way we get another piece of Him that we wouldn't have had otherwise.

What I want to be able to share with you now are the things God has woven into my life with incredible love and care and patience. Through the process of healing and recovery He has been working out these things in my own life, and I pray you will be encouraged and blessed by what I believe He has given me to give away.

This issue of forgiveness is one that I have had to really search out and come to terms with for myself, again and again (*Ugh! and again*). Though my experiences are not unique I have found that there is much misunderstanding and confusion on this subject, especially in the context of abuse and recovery.
It is my desire to simply share with you some of what I have learned over the course of my journey, and am continuing to learn more and more each day as I continue in my own process.

Because I grew up in an extremely abusive environment, I never knew that life could be safe, that people could be safe. Making mistakes and needing forgiveness certainly was not safe, and because of the nature of my abuse, I couldn't quite believe that God could be safe, either. I learned pretty early on, then, the importance of learning how to "do it right" and went to great extremes to make sure I did in order to survive in what was for me a very dark and violent world. I made hiding out an art, and pretending a profession. I obeyed "the rules" and kept all my secrets tucked far, far away, down deep inside, hidden even from myself. I lived within carefully constructed walls, not only to keep people out, but to keep me in, because I was so sure that I was so horrible and guilty and defiled and ruined, because I was convinced I deserved nothing better, because I was terrified that if people really saw me, really knew who I was, then they'd know, too - and that thought was absolutely unbearable.

As I began to really enter into the process and journey toward my healing, the forgiveness subject came up 'now and then.' My counselor began to 'imply' *(who, me?)* that perhaps this issue ought to be addressed - after all, he said, I had cause..., But then "forgiveness" was so easy at that point in my life - the pain never really touched me. I simply didn't let it. Because of "the rules" that I lived by I honestly couldn't see the need. Never complain, Never feel sorry for yourself, And NEVER get angry (especially at the ones whose job it is to hurt you!). Not only was it not safe, it was not practical. I really felt nothing about 'that kind of stuff' anyway. Unfortunately, I couldn't really feel much else, either.

When I was 17, however, I heard (or read, rather) for the first time the gospel of John. Jesus was telling His disciples that He was going away, "But I'm leaving you with a gift," He said, "peace of mind and heart, and the peace I give isn't like the peace of the world, so don't be troubled and afraid." It was there I found something that I knew I had wanted all my life. It was the promise of peace. *Peace - and no fear.* Hope began to spring up. Well, it didn't take long at all for me to respond to an invitation like that - I knew a good thing when I found it! and I grabbed it with all my might. I devoured the word. I couldn't wait to read the next chapter, that next verse. It was as if I were coming alive with it - literally (and I was).

Somehow I knew the answers to all my heart's yearning questions were there, the hope was there, light was there...

Unfortunately, though, so much that I longed to experience of the living God still eluded me, and the whole forgiveness thing evaded me. It was a concept I could not grasp. First of all, I couldn't quite believe it. I think I really felt I was beyond it - *NOT that I was too good for it, but that it was too good for me.* I was so full of despair and self-loathing and self-hatred that I didn't see how it could possibly apply in my case. I was absolutely convinced that all those sweet, lovely platitudes about God and His love, and the whole idea of redemption, somehow couldn't possibly apply or include me. It was all just too good to be true, too simple.

The even sadder part was, I didn't know why. I had no conscious memory at that time of my past or any clear picture of even my present. I just knew that I was bad, that I wasn't right, that I didn't measure up, and was too hopeless to believe I ever could. An incredible sadness pervaded and wrapped itself around me, but I couldn't acknowledge it. I was too well trained concerning "the rules." Being sad was not allowed, needing was not allowed, feeling was not allowed, and self-pity never was allowed. And needing comfort most certainly was not allowed.

And so, *The Walls* remained. As the years went by and I became more and more acquainted with the scriptures and involved with the body of Christ (at least the parts I knew) my discouragement at my internal condition only increased as my confusion over too many issues grew. I walked in perpetual condemnation. What I was hearing and reading and being told by the well-meaning people around me only added to my distress and outweighed my hope. Often I found that I couldn't reconcile the message and the Author of the Message, and my need for my self protective barriers grew right along with all those other things that were going on in my life.

Just Before Dawn

Here's the problem: How can a God that blames me and condemns me love and forgive me? How could a God that knows everything about me accept me? How could He even stand me with all my good intentions but never the capacity to see them through? And how could I dare to seek forgiveness when I had no other expectation than to fail and blow it all over again?

And, once I began to be able to admit the fact that I really had been hurt and violated, another dilemma arose - how could He ask me to forgive others when all it meant from my understanding on the subject was license to hurt me over and over again? After all, He didn't protect me, did He? How could He? Or why should He? In my mind I was entirely, completely worthless. What's the use?? I thought, *I lack the strength, I lack the faithfulness, I lack the faith...*

Where did I learn that - the belief that even in the Christian context I still wasn't acceptable? I suppose it was from people who were trying to figure out the same thing - and who would somehow compensate for that by constructing their own protective walls and barriers. Walls have names you know...(Isa. 60:15).

Only human walls don't always have such glorious names as those, our walls have names like, Pride, and Pretense, and Pain, and they serve a very specific purpose - that of keeping people out at a distance, making sure no one gets quite close enough to see what's really residing inside, like Doubt, Denial, Disillusionment, and whatever other inhabitants dwell within. We surround our walls with carefully constructed fences and gates - those are the rules and regulations we all live by (or at least do our best to follow) and others see that, don't they? And like God's people of old we forget what it means that <u>God alone</u> *is the Redeemer* for His people, and we fall into all kinds of traps and methods and means and ways to help *ourselves*, to fix *ourselves*, to make *ourselves* righteous and loudly demand that others do the same! How we miss out

Kicking the Walls

on the grace and mercy and love and kindness and patience and compassion of our God when we're in that "strength" mode!

Now where does the forgiveness thing come in and get all turned around the way it has? I suppose it goes back to the very beginning of time, even in the garden where Adam sinned and tried to cover *himself* by his own devices. It goes back to our understanding (or lack of it) as to what true forgiveness means or entails. I don't plan to go into guidelines and definitions of forgiveness with you, too many good people have already done that. What I want to share with you is the results of that - come around by the back door, so to speak, then we can decide for ourselves, with the Holy Spirit's help and direction, if this is something we really know about and are experiencing or not.

In the process of breaking down the walls of unforgiveness, we learn some vital lessons. Forgiveness is purifying. Forgiveness is freeing. Forgiveness is costly. While these lessons may seem wrong, contradictory, and impossible to achieve, we will explore them more deeply and find how God meant us to react and forgive, rather than how our abusers programmed us to submit and suffer.

The first result of true forgiveness is that it is purifying.
It brings me back into a place of restoration and fellowship *WITH GOD*, though not necessarily (not always) with the one I am forgiving. For example, you cannot tell an abuse survivor or someone who has been wounded deeply by the sinful actions of another that if they have truly forgiven then instantaneous love and longing for relationship and fellowship with that person will immediately occur! What my forgiving accomplishes *in me* is probably the most crucial part of the whole process. When I have come to a place where, with God's help, I can truly forgive another, the result for me is cleansing and purification before God. The bitter gall finally

stops assaulting my taste buds, and within the innermost parts of my being, a healing can take place because the wound stops festering at last. I find that at last I can walk forward and not need to cast angry glances behind me, and as a result I get along my way much faster than I did before.

<u>Another result of forgiveness is that it is freeing.</u>
Coming to the place of true, heartfelt, liberating forgiveness will require my whole heart's involvement. I cannot intellectualize at this point! Sitting at the feet of Jesus, I pour out my heart's store of pain and sorrow. I tattle to my Abba God. I verbalize the story so that together we can look over the whole sad, ugly picture, and then I listen as *He tells me back* (so to speak) what I am having to deal with and process, and then we come to terms together with these things. And when that really happens, I can leave it there, and I can start fresh all over again - not to allow those issues to repeat themselves, not to re-enter into the same destructive cycle of being hurt and have to go through this all over again, but to find a whole new path this time, the one that leads to health and freedom and holiness, the path that leads to wholeness, the one that leads me to Him!

<u>The third thing I want to point out about forgiveness is that it is costly.</u>
The reason I say this is because oftentimes it will require that I give up something I have held very 'dear' to me - especially if I've carried it around with me for a long time. After all, it's mine! I deserve it, I'm justified in feeling this way, and I have a right to it! (Don't I?) The struggle to relinquish this kind of (perceived) "control" can be so intense, so painful…and yet it is entirely worth working it through, however long it takes.

For some of us, remaining in denial has protected us for so long that we don't even know it's an issue, and when we do finally get to that place of owning and recognizing the incredible (at times) consequences of another's offenses against us, the implications of letting that go only seem to complicate the matter. *Denial is a double-edged sword, however. It "protects" us, but it also protects an entire system of false beliefs and misguided loyalties to our abusers* (who were often those of our own families). Our healing often means, then, disruption of the entire system, either in fact or in our misconceptions, and can bring about terrifying changes. For this, great courage will be needed.

What is an offense? *Strong's Exhaustive Concordance* translates that as, "a trap stick, like a bent sapling, a snare.
It is a cause of displeasure, an occasion to fall, a stumbling block." I Pet. 4:8 says that love covers the multitude of sins. Offenses. That word literally means, missing the mark (and, consequently, not sharing the prize), faults, errors, and trespasses. When I begin to recognize, to really enter in to what God says about forgiveness, and to let go of my denial and come to terms with those issues I need to do this work on, it will leave its mark on me. And it will change me, one way or another. When at last I willingly choose to relinquish my right to my pain and my anger it just might leave me aware of an incredible void for awhile. But only for a while, because God in His faithfulness waits, graciously and lovingly and patiently waits to fill it with Himself. Now that's worth the cost!

The thing I'm really learning about forgiveness, and knowing how to gauge when I'm walking in it, is by what I call *The Free Freedom Rule*. It was for freedom Christ set us free! (Gal. 5:1) *All* of us. Even the people that hurt me with their freedom. It is amazing to me how we can come to the place where we demand our freedom from others but aren't willing to give them theirs. Why? We're afraid. How do we know what that person will do with their freedom? Will they hurt me some more? Again? Still? Will they shame me? Hurt themselves? Destroy my reputation, take credit for my work, foul up my life in some irreparable way? Setting others free to

Just Before Dawn

choose takes things out of my control and places the responsibility where it belongs. I may not like all the possibilities that go along with this thinking, but it is the only way I know to get out of bondage. Set them free! When we do that we will finally have the freedom to walk in our own. Forgiveness does that for me. And it also gives God the freedom to be God both in my life and in the lives of those around me (Rom. 12:19).

Will there be consequences of giving people their freedom? Absolutely. But you and I then have the freedom to decide which of those consequences we are willing to live with, *or not*. That's God's gift of freedom *to us*.

How do we start? Perhaps with a simple prayer that goes something like this: "Most High God, I choose to forgive _____ for _____ and for making me feel _____." We must acknowledge both to ourselves and to God the consequences our abuser's (or whoever) actions brought upon us. We acknowledge the difficulty and pain this thing has caused us (and whoever else).

I also acknowledge the sin and hindrance this causes in my own life: bitterness - a sour taste, resentment - *anger on reserve!* (Now that's a hard one to let go of). Then I humbly relinquish control to God, Who alone can do all things. "Therefore, upon the basis of my faith in the Lord Jesus Christ and in dependence upon my God I give this person their freedom and determine by His help to walk in mine."

The responsibility has been shifted. I am the one who must make Godly choices. I must walk before my God and do whatever it takes to maintain my right standing and fellowship with Him. The prayer is complete when I pray, "O God, forgive *me!* I come to You for cleansing, Lord. I come to You in thankful worship for Your wonderful provision, for Your purifying redemption and renewal. I come to you for help and I seek You for transformation and change in the innermost part of me. I come to You now. Alone. O Father God, forgive me! Amen."

Unless we can honestly and in absolute, utter humility come to God in this way and with this level (or better) of reality, how can we as helpers in the healing process, or as seekers of healing for ourselves, ever hope to have anything of eternal value to pass on to those God brings into our lives or who meet us along life's way?

God Himself calls us, and draws us to Himself, on such terms, and ever waits with open arms for our response to His loving invitation.

May we discover the love and incredible grace of our forgiving God as we increasingly, experientially seek Him for restoration and hope and wholeness through the incredible power of forgiveness.

Rebuilding the Walls

"They will rebuild...and restore the places long devastated; they will renew the ruined cities that have been devastated for generations" (Isa. 61:4).

I love this verse, because it gives me so much hope that no matter how deep the devastation and desolation I feel within me, our God is a redeeming One, a restoring One. There is nothing too hard for Him, there is no pit too black and deep for Him to reach down into and rescue from. He has done it! And He will do it again and again for those who come to Him for healing and help and rescue.

"Thus says the Lord GOD: On the day that I cleanse you from all your iniquities, I will also enable you to dwell in the cities, and the ruins shall be rebuilt. The desolate land shall be tilled instead of lying desolate in the sight of all who pass by. So they will say, 'This land that was desolate has become like the garden of Eden; and the

wasted, desolate, and ruined cities are now fortified and inhabited.' Then the nations which are left all around you shall know that I, the LORD, have rebuilt the ruined places and planted what was desolate. I, the LORD, have spoken it, and I will do it" (Ezek 36:33-36 NKJV).

What hope! Could it possibly be that there really *is* light over there, just peeking over the horizon? It's so incredibly difficult to believe that daylight will indeed come when we're in the midst of the thick darkness that seems to penetrate every fiber of our being. "That's for other people. I'll never get there. It will always be like this." These are not uncommon thoughts and fears. Sometimes only the gaze of the Most High God can penetrate such darkness, but He remains faithfully nigh, watching, waiting, hoping that we will place our hand in His and receive His help and strength. We will get there - together with Him.

<u>Rebuilding My Jerusalem</u>
Becoming *more* than a survivor
By Diann

In the book of Nehemiah is the story about the rebuilding of the walls of Jerusalem. This story begins with a very descriptive account of the ruin and desolation as reported to and observed by Nehemiah. For me, this account parallels the healing journey of the abuse victim.

In chapter one, verse three it says, "The survivors who are left from the captivity in the province are there in *great distress and reproach*." Those words pretty well describe "survivors." They also let us know how important it is to become more than just a survivor. Survivors of any trauma are initially in a state of 'great distress and reproach."

I could so clearly identify with this band of Jews who had escaped their captivity. They had survived their ordeal, but nothing more. It was evident to anyone who looked at them that they were in distress. The survivors bore the reproach of their captivity.

We must allow God to heal our wounds and move us out of the pain of our past. That does not mean we shove it down and pretend it never happened. It means we deal with it openly and honestly. That means we talk about it with the safe people in our lives, and we allow the Holy Spirit to go deep inside our souls to show us what is there. It is not an easy journey. It means having to walk back through some very unpleasant things. We do that in order to be healed, not to cast blame upon others, but in order for the Holy Spirit to heal our wounds. We all have tried, in one way or another, to put our abusive past behind us and move on with life, but until the wounds are dealt with properly, moving on cannot happen. Sometimes entire foundations of our lives have to be rebuilt, just like Nehemiah did for the city of Jerusalem.

God specializes in restoration. Isaiah 54:4 says, *"Do not fear, for you will not be ashamed; neither be disgraced, for you will not be put to shame; for you will forget the shame of your youth..."* The fear and shame that I lived with and struggled under for so long are gone. I am now in a continual process of restoration as God helps me discover the person He created me to be.

One night my husband gave me a beautiful sapphire ring. As I was getting ready for bed, I told the Lord, "I really love this ring! It seems so special." Now the ring was special to me simply because it came as a surprise gift from my husband, but it seemed to go far beyond that.

God quickly directed me to Revelation 21 and impressed the phrase "the new Jerusalem" into my mind. As I began to read the scriptures, I was overwhelmed. *"The foundations of the wall of the city were adorned with all kinds of precious stones: the first foundation was jasper, the second sapphire..."*
(Rev. 21:19).

Just Before Dawn

God was giving me a new foundation upon which to rebuild the walls of my life. He had given me the sapphire ring (through my husband) as a token of His covenant with me. God was saying to me "Give me all that you are and I will give you all that I AM." What an exchange! I give Him all the ruin in my life and He gives me all of Himself!

Now, returning to our story in Nehemiah:
"The wall of Jerusalem is also broken down and its gates are burned with fire." The walls of the city were its protection. Jerusalem was in ruin and had become a laughingstock. It was a vulnerable and unprotected city.

Verse 4 continues, *"So it was, when I heard these words, that I sat down and wept, and mourned for many days; I was fasting and praying before the God of heaven."*
Discovering or "seeing" the truth about the abuse is a very difficult step in recovery. I was one of those people who had pushed most of the trauma of my abuse down inside my soul. Part of the process of being healed is allowing the Holy Spirit to bring out whatever He desires for us to see and to know. It is not a digging up of past hurts and sorrows for the sake of remembering all the terrible things that happened to us, but it is coming out of denial into the light of God's truth. Seeing that truth will cause weeping and mourning. Seeing the truth causes us to realize that our lives are in ashes.

In Isaiah 61:3 & 4 we find these words: *"To console those who mourn in Zion, to give them beauty for ashes, the oil of joy for mourning, the garment of praise for the spirit of heaviness; that they may be called trees of righteousness, the planting of the Lord, that He may be glorified."*

In Isaiah 54:11 we find these words, *"O you afflicted one, tossed with tempests, and not comforted, Behold, I will lay your stones with colorful gems and lay your foundations with sapphires."*

Kicking the Walls

The foundation of my life was in such ruin, that God covenanted with me to lay a second foundation. My part of the covenant was to give Him the rubble of the first foundation. That involves letting go of the wrong done to me and turning loose of the pain and sorrow.

God has repeatedly shown Himself to be intimately concerned about my life. He has shown me in many ways how much He wants to heal and restore me. All that is required of me is to bring Him all of my woundedness and pain. I give Him the ashes of my life and He gives me His beauty. I bring Him my sorrow and mourning and He gives me His joy. I bring Him the spirit of a heavy heart and He clothes me with the garment of praise. He plants my life in fertile soil so that I may grow strong in Him, that He may be glorified. All praise and honor and glory to Him forever and ever!

Allowing the truth to be revealed as we come out of denial, mourning the losses of our lives, owning our ashes (accepting the truth), and then trading those ashes to God for the beauty He promised, are all steps of restoration.

Isaiah 61:4: *"And they shall rebuild the old ruins, they shall raise up the former desolations, and they shall repair the ruined cities, the desolation of many generations."*
The ruins of our lives can be rebuilt, the desolations can be raised up, and the ruined cities repaired.

Some of us are so adept at wall building that not only have we enclosed ourselves within them, we have built up well fortified cities, walls within walls! This next piece typifies the extent that some of us have gone to in our desperate attempts for survival.

Just Before Dawn

The City

*The walls had been broken down
the boundaries all crossed
while the city was young
And the constant plundering
of what should have been her treasure store
produced only barrenness and loss
Her would-be-glorious light was dimmed
her would-be-life snuffed out
The teeming crowds were denied access
loneliness and desolation taking their place
Who hears the silent scream
or comforts her despair?*

*Then One came
Who had seen the city's fall
and mourned her losses
He drew near and looked upon her ruins
and determined that the time for rebuilding had come
He set His plan for restoration in progress
and the long task was begun*

*Many of the dwelling places inside had to be
broken down completely and built again
In every place the foundation had to be made sure
Then the work in earnest began
Bit by bit and piece by piece
one stone upon another
each piece fitting together perfectly
so that never again could she be breached
He saw to every detail of her remaking
'til her restoration made her stronger and more glorious a place
than ever could have been possible before*

This describes the healing process, at least in part. How quickly we become frustrated that things just aren't getting better fast enough,

Kicking the Walls

that somehow we must be behind some schedule (even though there is no such thing) and should be "done" by this time…We must ask ourselves this, though; how long does it take for a solid foundation to be laid? If we should choose to build upon an old and cracked one, no matter how beautiful and costly the materials are, no matter how skilled the craftsman who builds is, still it will not stand the test of time, it will not endure the inevitable storms of life that will certainly beat upon it. Have patience, it is well worth the wait!

At last it became fit for the King Himself to dwell there
and He does
Her dark places have been flooded with Light the streets made smooth
and free
In the heart of the city is set the throne room of the Highest
With His presence come hope and peace and safety
Expectation and breathless anticipation
at His spoken word
The sounds of life are in the air

Sometimes the enemies encamp without the walls
and seek to do her harm
who want to undo the work
But they are powerless to reclaim her
the King's own treasured possession
the dwelling place of the Most High

The watchmen are upon the walls
and as long as they remain and are vigilant
She is safe
For the enemies without know that the Captain of the Lord of Hosts is
within
awaiting any summons or call to arms
He is a faithful Defender and Friend

It is indeed wonderful to bask in those victories we experience along the way, and to rejoice at the progress we make in our healing, and yet we often become discouraged when we still feel the old sadness creep up now and then. The belief that the feelings of grief and sadness should no longer affect us ever again are simply not true. It is right to grieve. It will get better, honest, but it will take time, and that's ok.

But at times the city is sadness
She weeps
Why do you still mourn your losses, O city?
See the wonderful work the King has performed within thee!

The fountains flow with the tears from my bottles
stored these many years by Him on my behalf
It is allowed
He will never forget my desolation
or the destruction they brought upon me
To mourn at times is allowed
and does not lessen the rebuilding He has done
but deepens its meaning
and heightens its worth

I have loved thee, O city,
and set My mark upon thy doorposts
My seal upon thy gates
Never again will cruel men mar thee
nor the destroyer enter in to bring thy death
Life is My gift to thee
Receive it
Live
Be renewed
Grow
And I will walk in thee
Thy streets shall be My constant highways
Many will be brought to thee
and health and healing shall happen within these walls
New life will flow into all who enter in through the gates
The blessing of the Most High shall be upon thee

Kicking the Walls

and the light of the King of Kings Himself
shall shine within thee

O thou city of God, thou art Mine!
My own dwelling place
Dare to rejoice and be glad, little one
for the Lord Himself doth love thee
and will ever keep thee
And this proclamation shall stand forever
and for all time Amen
and shall not be undone
for the mouth of the Lord Himself
has spoken it concerning thee
even thee!

Nothing can steal us out of His hand! Though the thought of "owning" our pain and hopelessness is not an easy one, doing so is a key to healing and restoration. It is true that we cannot give away what we do not possess. The difficulty for many of us is that denial seems so much safer, so much more tolerable. And so we remain there, sadly, and cannot get beyond our pain. We have no idea what restoration looks like. It is often at this point that many of us find ourselves propelled into the next stage of the journey:

Enter, *The Process.*

Just Before Dawn

What's back there?

<u>Missing Pieces</u>
In memory of RaLynne

So many the missing pieces
So many the untold tale
That a picture cannot be painted
Surely to try 'twould but fail!
What is absent speaks far louder
Than that which has already been shown
Wielding a power far greater
Because they are yet unknown

*Prisoner of Childhood
By Tara*

Just Before Dawn

The Process

What can we do, o'er whom the unbeholden
Hangs in a night with which we cannot cope?
What but look sunward, and with faces golden
Speak to each other softly of a Hope?
(Margaret Clarkson)

In this section we'd like to focus on the *healing* process. What is it that leads (or rather, drives) us into *The Process?* For many of us, it is certainly not something we would have chosen on our own! Were it not for the intense pressure and desperation for relief that driving us to seek help many of us would continue on with our lives as if nothing had ever happened to cause such internal pain and distress. Why bother? Apart from the hope that light will eventually pierce the thick darkness so that we can walk in the light of healing, there would be no point to doing so at all. For the child of God, it is He that is the deciding factor.

"But God..."

Alone, we walk with our private pain,
Clutching a sadness we cannot explain,
Mourning our losses, bowed by our grief,
Blind to all hope, void of relief.

Unseen fetters binding us fast
from some dark corner back in the past...

How long remain hidden these specters of woe?
Deep in that darkness I know I must go,
open the crypts full of death and decay,
exposing their secrets to the light of the day.

When will relief come and stay as a friend?
When will the agony come to an end?
How long 'til I no longer struggle to keep

The Process

> *my sanity, sanctity? When will I reap*
> *that constant rest others seem to enjoy?*
> *unharried by voices that seek to destroy,*
> *to undo, to frighten, to rob of all life...*
> *O what is it like to rest from the strife?!*

The point in entering into the process is all about hope - finding it if you have lost it, discovering it if you have never had it at all. Hope is essential in order for us to be able to function and endure. When we are without hope, even the thought of getting up in the morning can be a major challenge, and seeing the process through will be nearly impossible. The Bible tells us that "hope deferred makes the heart sick." It confirms the fact that God, Who is Himself hope, is deeply invested in bringing us to the place of hope in order that we might walk in health and wholeness and in the abundance He intended for us from the beginning.

> *But for the pastures and healing streams,*
> *and the visions of hope as I gaze on my King,*
> *and but for the balm that He pours on my wounds,*
> *and for the hope that I have in His Son,*
> *but for the Word that He speaks in my ear,*
> *and for the strong arms upholding and near,*
> *the price of the conflict is too a great cost,*
> *for but for the Healer, all hope would be lost!*
> *My life would be forfeit, my ruin be sure,*
> *my pain would be more than life could endure,*
> *devastation undo me, trouble increase,*
> *the sorrow consume me, my usefulness cease...*
>
> *I thank Thee, O God, for the call to endure,*
> *that the end of all trial and conflict is sure,*
> *that at last in my Lord Christ triumphant I'll rise,*
> *receive from His own hand the crown and the prize,*
> *bask in His presence, all mourning long past,*
> *and entering into that long rest at last,*

*declare with the angels the love of the King
that rescued a captive, and taught her to sing!*

For those of us who are afraid to hope we have good news: Healing *is* possible! Wholeness *is* attainable! Life *is* worth doing, because the Source of all hope doesn't change and will not abandon us to hopelessness.

Sharon is one survivor who chose to enter into the process by necessity. Because she remained in and walked through it she can write from the perspective of one who has gleaned much hope and can walk in that hope on a daily basis.

> I know what I have survived and I know how I have survived it all, but I am just beginning to learn why I have survived. Only recently have I begun to realize who God is and how Jesus fits into it all. Before, I could have written a very moving woe-is-me tale that would have evoked emotions and sympathies from a "target audience." However, there would have been a shallowness, a hollowness, descriptive yet empty words. Yet, I could not have come to this realization about God without having gone through the emptiness: a circuitous route but not a never-ending loop. At some point I did step out of the circular rut. Had I not pushed and struggled through the healing process, I would still be clinging to the lies and misconceptions that kept me from pursuing Him.
>
> I had heard of God being a father. Why in the world would I want another father? Behind his mask of benevolence, the earthly father I had was manipulative, deceitful, selfish, never satisfied, never approving, not honorable, and not trustworthy. Wouldn't God just be the same on a universal scale? As a child of my biological father, I had no power, no voice, no choice and no escape. Why revel in being a child of a Heavenly Father Who is omnipotent, omniscient, Who chose

The Process

me, "before the foundation of the world," and Who would be my ultimate, eternal judge?

Yet, something propelled me through the muck and mire and the sludge of despair. I think it was faith. The hope in something I could barely visualize, the possibility of an outside chance to experience freedom. It was a mere glimmer of a better way. An easing of the pain would have been sufficient; I never dared to think that freedom from it was even possible. A taste of life would have been enough; a glimpse of Heaven was more than I dreamed of.

But, here I am, today. Am I healed? I am scarred. I bear the effects of abuse in my mind and in my body. Like a physical malady that required surgery, there was intense pain that caused me to cry out for help. Even though the help itself proved to be painful, it was pain that lead to healing rather than degenerating to deeper harm. Recovery has been long with occasional setbacks, slight relapses now and then. Overall, at this end of the healing path, the memory of the hurt is fading, just like the scars from surgery. I am no longer a victim; I am a survivor.

The question remains: Am I healed? I am definitely better and healthier, but the scars testify to a time when things were worse. Are they constant reminders? No. Still, if one gets bumped or poked, I become aware of where they came from. I have discovered that, even in His resurrected body, Jesus still bore the scars of His crucifixion. Did He need them as a reminder of what He had endured? Not likely. They were, however, a touch point for others, a visible symbol of the process He suffered in order to not only redeem us, but to prove that He understands us by having become one of us.

I can apply the example of Christ by coming alongside another survivor of abuse and comforting with the comfort I have received. Without my scars, I would have no credibility and no testimony. Because of Jesus, His love for me, and His

Just Before Dawn

obedience to God's plan, I can say with confidence that *there is hope* and healing and I am alive because God is good.

Hope

What is hope? And how will having hope sustain us through the long nighttime of pain? Even more than a want or a wish for something, *hope is an expectation, anticipation, a deep desire, a confident trust.* Without it, we cannot endure, and life will seem pointless and intolerable.

Now we must each ask ourselves: on what does *my* hope lie?
If you are in a time of darkness and distress, your hope may be as straightforward as hoping the pain will stop - soon!

Perhaps this is a good place to really think about *The Process*.
What is meant by "the process" and what does it look like?

According to Webster's Dictionary, *a process is a course, steps, or methods towards a desired result.* For each of us, regardless of our backgrounds and personal histories, the process involves becoming whole people. EVERYONE is in process, because none of us has been made complete and whole yet. No one can look at life and say, "Well, I'm done! I'm perfect now, I've finally got it all together!" No one has arrived, we are ALL on the journey towards being conformed into the likeness of Jesus Christ. For some of us, however, the process is just more complex, more intense - but only because we are much more aware than the majority of what the healing process entails!

God is a God of process. For some reason He chose to create the earth one day at a time, though He certainly didn't have to. In that process of creation, God set into motion a basic law of nature, which ALL of creation is subject to. God began by making clear distinctions between one thing and another: divided night from day, darkness from light, etc. (Gen 1:3, 6, 9). Then God began to build upon and multiply upon those things (Gen 1:11).

The Process

He began to expand His creation (Gen 1:14) but also to prepare it for what in the future would be needed. God had already factored man into the creation plan. Because God is timeless He didn't need stars and seasons to mark its passage, but He knew we would, as a measuring stick of sorts. You see, *there was purpose in every step God took in the process - and there is meaning and value and wisdom and purpose in ours, as well.* We CAN trust God for the process!

Next, He created us in His image and then entrusted to us some of His own attributes, like the ability to govern, to enhance the creation, so to speak, by using the special gifts and abilities that only the human part of creation uniquely possessed over the rest of what God made (Gen 1:26-7).

Gen 2:5 points out that at that point in the process, "there was not a man to till the ground." God didn't send the rain, which would give the ground the capacity to produce, *until it was time.* The Genesis account reminds us that from the very, very beginning, God had a purpose for man, and it's when we don't feel we have one that hopelessness and discouragement become overpowering. Those, and all the "why" questions, begin to have power to overwhelm us and rob us of our joy. Work was not a result of the curse, it was a part of the dignity God always meant for us to walk in as co-helpers with Him; it was meant to be one of the things that God gave for us to be able to share in the joy and satisfaction that God had in His work of creation.

God understood the consequences that the process of time and its ravages would have on us, and He's very interested in our life processes. He is deeply concerned - and engaged with us - in how those processes have affected us. This includes how our past experiences have affected us, as well. How do we, for example, deal with our feelings of deep inadequacy, or the belief that we are ruined, marred, damaged goods based on our past experiences and ways of coping? This next article by Robyn describes in allegory what many of us feel:

Just Before Dawn

Jewel Box

The chest of drawers sits in the corner, covered with dust. I haven't looked in it for years; actually, I usually avert my eyes so I won't see it at all. This chest is an elephant in my existence that I try to ignore, a symbol of my sickness and despair. It is the essence of my life, the pith of my heart.

It is large, made out of pine. The workmanship is bad; it stands out of balance, leaning toward destruction, teetering forward with every tremor. Wondering if it can ever be repaired, I look closely and remember trying to polish the chest, trying to make it presentable. I have used lots of polish and rubbed really hard but I just cannot get the luster to come through. I realize that I lacked the knowledge and wisdom of a true carpenter and the proper tools with which to construct this chest.

Nevertheless, that is past and looking into the deep drawers, I see what is stored inside. See this? It's the necklace I wear whenever I feel inadequate. Yes, it's quite heavy, kind of ugly, isn't it? At the bottom of the chain is a wide piece of metal with a heart shaped stone. The stone is not quite the pure red of a real ruby, for I could not afford the real thing. It looks pretty good at first glance but then I realize that the setting is broken and the stone is ready to fall out. I also see the scratches that have come from years of abuse - the abuse of being laughed at and pushed around, the abuse of my anger as I would throw it back into the drawer, enraged that this would not protect me from the arrows directed at my heart. I will just place it over here on the table until I am able to look and decide which pieces need to be kept or thrown away.

Why am I doing this? Tell me again, why must I examine the junk in these drawers?
Oh, yes, it is because the container is full and the pieces fail quite often in their intended purpose.

The Process

This next drawer sticks, but I manage to wrench it open to reveal a collection of rings. They have a double use, to draw your eye away from the inner me and to deflect life's blows. This first band is plain, as you can see. I wear this ring most often, using it to prevent me from being controlled by others. I have learned that being out of control is to be hurt. It is to be abused in every way: physically, mentally, and sexually. I cannot allow myself to ever be hurt again. This ring reminds me to show disinterest in your opinions, apathy toward your passions, and indifference toward your pain. I am able to be at my opinionated and arrogant best when I don this circle that acts as a shackle on my heart. I am just starting to realize that when I deny you your passions and outlook I obstruct my own craving to be recognized as the warm and loving person I really am. It just has not been safe to show that side of me.

The next ring is another favorite - it is my birthstone, topaz. It is a yellow stone that reflects the fear of your anger. You see I wear it to remind myself to never rock the boat, never show my real feelings that are contradictory to yours. To risk your ire is to throw myself in front of a speeding train letting the wheels of your fury sever me from my soul. Cowering behind this ring protects me from the shriek of your rage.

The next drawer is full of earrings. There are so many different pairs - each style draws the eye of the beholder so that my eyes will never have to meet theirs. I dislike people who try to look deeply inside of my soul; I fear being seen as I am, for I am afraid that I am not enough. This first pair is interesting - they are little jesters! See the silly hat sitting on top of the face that is forever frozen in a funhouse smile? These are my earrings of self-contempt. They are very useful when I am feeling inadequate; I can divert your attention away from an area that cannot bear the fresh pain of my interpretation of your judgment. That is why I cannot see and feel your words as they are given, for I must first filter them through the dirty cheesecloth of my memory, comparing them

Just Before Dawn

to past instances that allowed the sarcasm of others to stomp on the deep and fragile inner me.

Here's an earring that has no mate. You might ask why I would only want a single bobble to adorn myself, making me unbalanced and lop-sided. The answer is really very easy; this is the piece I wear when I long for a relationship with another person. No matter if I desire friendship or a more intimate type of interaction, this single scrap of jewelry reminds me that it is safer to be alone, never having to worry about being hurt.

I used to have two, but now I hang on to this single souvenir as a reminder of how much pain is entailed when the pair is split, the sword of betrayal hacking the twain, coming between the whole of the relationship in the violent deception of a self-serving partner; the partner who, with a dagger of trust, was capable of severing my open heart from my soul. It reminds me that I will never again have to berate myself for the naiveté of believing that someone could love me as much as I love him. I will never have to relive that poignant bitter-sweetness which is to have loved and lost. Weighted, I use its heaviness to pull me down into the depths of my innermost being, reminding myself that there is safety in single numbers, even if there is no joy.

Oh! Look! Look at these…they are so precious to me, these wide disks of shiny silver. They are symbols of my perfectionism and self-sufficiency. I made them myself, you know, sitting down amid the raw material that was once the center of myself and pounding them out. Blow by blow, the hammer rained down upon the metal, each dent blending in with the last to form a uniform, if bumpy, exterior. I hammered them with the mallet that is my fear of rejection and I polished them with my pride until they looked lustrous and the light reflects off of them in such a way that distracts your attention from the knowledge that I know I cannot do this alone. I keep these close by so that I may work on them

The Process

whenever I begin to feel susceptible in any way that suggests that I need help. Even though they tarnish easily, I keep polishing in the hope that one day I will finally be able to say, "I'm okay." If you look closely, there are dimples in the surface but I'll keep working on them so that someday they will be perfect and I won't have to worry about anyone seeing the damage of rejection in my life.

Here is another set; gold-tone hoops that I wear to adorn the part of me I have created to reflect you. They set off the new part of me I have built so that I can be exactly what you want. I wear these to show my need for your acceptance, for I am a quick-change artist, and chameleon-like, I can change the passion of my heart at your very whim. Like to hike? Me too! Would you rather sit in front of the television watching Star Trek reruns? Me too! Gee, you want to sit in a bar and direct your blurry stare into my eyes while I listen to you insisting that you love me for who I am? Well, okay. I can sit and listen to your lies. Just let me change myself to come into line with the needs of your soul. Funny, I never noticed that the hue of the gold is wearing thin here and there. Seemingly, there is something underneath the gold plating - it's plastic! Just plain old plastic. Hmmm.

There's more in this drawer but nothing that is really important - just little pieces of me that I have used from time to time. Fragments of my identity that are interchangeable and deflect your gaze. I'll just dump the rest of the contents over here in a pile. Looking, I see that the resulting tangle of tarnished finery is no more a true composite of myself than is each piece separately. They are all bits of the lie of my existence.

Some of these items have been with me all my life, a few are heirlooms passed down from generation to generation. I know I need to clean this chest out and get rid of the rubble that fills it. I just can't seem to part with it, though. What will I do? Jesus has promised me comfort, has promised to restore my soul; He says He will give me joy and the voice of singing, if I let Him. Do I dare? Do I let Him journey deep into my heart and start cleaning out the past pains that cling to the innermost parts of me? To do so will cause pain upon pain as the lies, like ivy being torn off brick walls, coming loose from the essence of my being. I long to let myself invite the warmth of the Sonshine to heal the inner me. I would love to accept the love that the Jeweler of the Universe offers; I would love to don the new jewelry that will replenish my soul. I look forward to that day. Do I dare hope for more than I have? My ways have worked for so long, not very well, but they have worked. Can I...? Should I...? Will I...?

What a great picture of our many ways of "adorning" ourselves! Why do we believe this is so necessary? For too many of us, we find ourselves living under the tyranny of fear of people - people's opinion, approval, and acceptance. Only in exchanging our allegiance to the God Who unreservedly receives us as we are will we be free from such an existence.

Truth

One verse that has been incredibly misunderstood by so many is, "forgetting what lies behind," in Phil. 3:13. Somehow we get the idea that looking at our past issues in order to resolve the internal conflicts raging within us is wrong. What took place in our past is, however, relevant both to our present and to our future. Our past experiences have shaped us into who we are today. While we certainly need to remain as "present" as we can and live and sow here for the future, it is in learning from the past that we can often glean the very resources that will provide for a future harvest of brand new things. If we are wise, we will allow the lessons from the past to help grow from what we learn as a result of it.

Let's look at a passage in Gen. 16, where God meets one of His people in the desert. He asks her some very pointed questions:

The Process

In verse 7, God asks, *"Hagar, servant of..."* God recognized her present circumstances, and acknowledged where she was. *"Where have you come from?"* He's interested in her past experiences, and asks, How did you get here, Hagar? Tell Me what brought you to this place. Yes, God already knew, but God also knew that Hagar needed to know that He knew, to voice it out loud. She needed to be able to speak the hurts and concerns and difficulties and burdens upon her heart. God knew that because God created her that way - just as He created us that way, and even goes out of His way to provide for that need to be met in His people. God is never distressed about our seeking Godly counsel (Prov. 11:14) and asking questions, or our need to find some answers, understanding, significance, or relief. In fact, He invites it, asking us again and again to come to Him to seek His face (Isa. 55:3), to ask Him the hard questions (Ps. 2:8), to tell Him about our hurts and confusion, and to come to terms with the things we need to resolve (Isa. 45:19). He wants us to admit to the things that trip us up and cause us pain, that trigger intense feelings, that lead us down the path of despair and leave us reeling with feelings of helplessness and frustration and defeat (Matt.11:28, Jn. 7:37). Remember that Moses, and David, Elijah, Job, and too many others to list here, dared to ask God the hard questions, and came away with a greater knowledge and understanding of Him that could not have been attained in any other way (Job 42:5). The True Lord Jesus Himself is the merciful and compassionate High Priest, the One Who makes intercession for us, the One Who is acquainted with our grief and sorrows and pain (Heb. 2:17,18, Isa. 53:3). We can, then, freely come to Him openly and honestly with our hard questions, knowing that His is a throne of grace, not judgment, that we come before (Heb. 4:16).

Now the next question God asked: *"And whither wilt thou go?"* So, Hagar, what now? Where to from here? How will you respond to this situation? Which choice? For we certainly DO have choices (and that's the difference between bondage and freedom), no matter what it seems like at the moment. Which choice will best help us in seeing God's will and direction and plan for our lives accomplished?

Maybe we don't have all the answers. Maybe we don't have all the information right now (Okay, so we seldom have those things!) but we can certainly seek out the God Who does. *Because we know His character, and that He is not only able, but willing to help us to walk in hope and confidence and to rest and peace and joy, we can seek God for these things!* We really can expect that there is a remedy for whatever circumstance and situation we find ourselves in, and there is a vision and a perspective we perhaps have not seen before (or maybe just forgotten in our distress). God IS faithful, and will always make a way, one way or another, because He is God.

Prov. 4:18 says, *"But the path of the uncompromisingly just and righteous is like the light of dawn, that shines more and more - brighter and clearer - until it reaches its full strength and glory in the perfect (full light of) day"* (Amp).

God is God of heaven's economy, where giving away for Him means increase and plenty in return, where relinquishing to Him paltry things brings about a transformation of (into) richness and plenty and abundance. *That's* what God is like!

"For I know the thoughts and plans that I have for you, says the Lord, thoughts and plans for welfare and peace, and not for evil, to give you an expectation of hope in your future" (Jeremiah 29:11 Amp).

Confidence

Sometimes, the very greatest act of faith and the most precious gift that we can give to both God and to ourselves is in coming to the place of decision - where we decide that *God in His Sovereignty and infinite wisdom knows all about what He's all about.* We must determine to remain determined, and rest in the confident hope that the God Who knows all things, the One Who created us, is more than competent. He is able to bring us to that desired end. He is working, working on our behalf, in us, through us, for us, because of (or sometimes, we must admit) in spite of us and our own efforts to do it ourselves.

The Process

Let's pray for one another that God, the God Who honors *the process*, quickly brings us to this place in our own process, in cooperation with Him, and in unity with His plan and purpose, so that we may be fully equipped and prepared and have the capacity for the incredibly even greater things that He has in store for us!

Coping

This next narrative actually took place several years ago, at a time I was strongly questioning so many things in my life, and doubting the whole "process thing" (as I so despondently called it).

I just wasn't sure it was all worth it, I wasn't convinced. But then that day came, the day I saw things about *the process* from an entirely new perspective. That's when I wrote about the diamond.

The Secret of the Diamond

What a year this has been! How acutely aware I have been of the peaks and valleys as never before, the lessons taught there, the emotions of it all - it seems the heights have been higher and more glorious than at any other time in my life, but the depths have been deeper, too, more painfully felt and experienced, but then the deliverances more wonderful and worshipful, too. What a strange, awesome, difficult mix of it all, and what a privilege to have been led here. And how glad I am for the One Who changes not, however my circumstances may. I can't help but look expectantly for what ever awaits around the next corner! I feel both anticipation and reluctance, mixed in with excitement and reserve. What will it be like ahead?

God has been teaching me lately about diamonds and the processes that form them, and as always I am surprised by His joy in the learning of it. What a wise and wonderful teacher

Just Before Dawn

He is! Our God uses even the very processes of nature to instruct us in His ways and to reveal to us His own sovereignty and glory. *"For since the creation of the world His invisible nature and attributes, that is, His eternal power and divinity have been made intelligible and clearly discernible in and through the things that have been made - His handiworks" (Rom. 1:20 Amp).*

This lesson began one morning as I was driving to work. I was praying one of my typical rushing to-work-stressing-out-prayers. I finally whined, "Lord, You've just got to do something about this pressure in my life! I just know I'm going to crack up any day now!" (or something along those lines). Anyway, I arrived at the shop, pulled myself together as best I could, and got to work. Not long after the store opened a customer walked in with a four-carat diamond for consignment. After he left, the shop owner came to show me the gem and told me how to look for the characteristics of the diamond that determine its value. "Yes, this one is practically flawless," he said, "there are just a few tiny carbon specks here and there. Take a look." It looked perfect to me! Even with the help of the magnifying glass I couldn't see them at first. All I saw was beauty and glitter. It was magnificent. Then I saw them - practically undetectable amidst all those sparkles, but there.

"Whatever made those black specks?" I asked him. "How did they get there?"

"Oh, well, that's all diamonds are in their first state, just black clumps of carbon. *It's pressure that makes a diamond.* Prolonged periods of extreme pressure are what transforms coal and causes it to become a diamond. God does it."

O.K. Lord, I'm listening!

Over the next hour or so I learned many other things about the diamond. I was absolutely fascinated as I studied it, enthralled

The Process

by its beauty. "What makes it sparkle so? Is that part of the stone?" I asked him.

"Oh, no." he said, "It's the cuts in the diamond, called facet cuts, that reflect the light and make it such a thing of beauty." I read later that a diamond has special optical properties that guarantee its preeminence among gems because of its high refractive index, or light bending ability, *that enables it to throw back almost all the light that enters* a well-cut gem. Facet cutting uses smooth, flat faces, which are cut into the gem at *precise* angles so that the greatest amount of light is refracted. Gem cutting is an art that, when done by an expert master craftsman, is able to transform rough gems and bring out to the fullest its greatest beauty and highest value. *The best-proportioned ones throw back the most light.* I realized, too, that though it sparkled and shone from every direction, *the diamond was loveliest when viewed from directly above.* In other words, the fullest effect of all those facet cuts, their size, shape, placement, was most stunning when viewed from the top looking down into the heart of the stone.

"What about the size?" was my next question. "Why is a stone this size so valuable? Is it rare to find one like it or just plain expensive?"

"To find a cut stone this size is indeed rare, which is why it is so expensive." he said. "You see, diamonds are usually found *by sifting*, and then only twenty percent of those mined are suitable for gemstones. When they do get to the cutter he then determines how much of a cut and which size and type the stone will bear. He familiarizes himself with it and learns the way 'the grain' runs before he sets to work. The finished product is so much smaller than when he begins because most stones crumble into smaller pieces when they are cut, *and yet no part of it goes to waste.* The diamond is such a hard stone that even its powder has usefulness."

It's the pressure that makes the diamond. The words kept racing through my mind all day long. I felt so awed as I considered it all, and I felt a little afraid, too. *The price is too high!* Clay I can do, but a diamond?! I can't do it. I don't think I want to do it. I won't do it!

I paced. I pined. I pouted. I stomped my little foot!

I relented. I repented. I rested. And I remembered...

God's will __will__ be accomplished in my life, despite me and my abilities (and/or lack of them). That was an issue we had settled long ago, God and I. He would be God in my life, in every issue and area of it, He the Master, I His servant. The roles were established and would not be changed. I will not question Him or seek to change His mind. *Thou alone art God!*

O.K. Lord, I'm watching, I'm waiting.

After two days I went back to the schoolroom and seated myself right back down at the feet of the Teacher, and I'm learning as I watch and attend to His movements in and around me. He has wonders to share, and I ask myself how I could ever doubt His plan and wisdom, or consider any other way better.

There must be a secret to all this! Perhaps there's some key that will unlock vast hidden treasures? Even diamonds are formed in dark and hidden places. *Tell me, Master, what is the secret of the diamond?*

Then I realized it. *The secret is not in and of the diamond itself, but in the sovereignty of the Creator of the diamond.* The diamond does nothing but wait out the long processes of nature and become what it was intended to be *by remaining* so that the process can be completed. The more complete the process the purer the diamond. Yes, the process can be interrupted. It can be hindered. It can be altered. Only if it remains where it is set can coal become diamond.

As for me, I'm not moving, O God! I will be still. Help me, enable me, cause me to endure. I am so weak. May Thy strength be perfected here in even me!

Is pressure more pleasant to me now? Do I like it? No way! But I'm learning to trust the wisdom and judgment of the Father Who applies it - or the use of it - in a new way, and I'm amazed as I see His hand in it, and the benefits I'm reaping cannot be taken away. Pressure has a way of bringing up and out of us things we may not have known were down inside. It reveals to us, if we are honest, the truth about ourselves, and leads us to new revelations of the truth about our God - the kind of truth that sets us free.

So, I'm listening carefully, I'm watching, I'm waiting, I'm gleaning every grain I can find and I'm storing it up in a basket. And when it finally all lets up, as I know it must, God will have something to show for it, something worthy of praise for His master craftsmanship, a gemstone worthy to adorn the crown of a King. A diamond!

Even me, O God, let it be me!

"*We were under great pressure, far beyond our ability to endure, so that we despaired even of life. Indeed, in our hearts we felt the sentence of death. But this happened that we might not trust and rely on ourselves but on God, Who raises the dead*" (II Cor. 1:8 and 9).

We all get tired and grow weary of the process, but we can bear it if only we have hope. What happens, though, when we lose our hope? God is certainly the restorer of it, but before that healing work begins in us we must try to get along in whatever way we can in order to cope, to survive until hope comes. That's how coping mechanisms are developed.

Just Before Dawn

<u>Coping Mechanisms</u>

When we were children, for example, small and defenseless, without choices, without safety, and without hope of relief, what then? What lengths did we have to go to in order to survive until healing could begin? Often, that depends on the type and severity of the abuse we were forced to endure.

While God has given each man and woman the freedom to choose what they will do with their freedom, He does not abandon us who are wounded by the evil choices of others, and He does not leave us without a way to cope, to bear up under it. Depending upon our need, God supplies methods, ways, and means, in order for life to be preserved until we can finally employ *our own* free will and enter into the healing process. When sorrow and pain and injustice and cruel abuse cannot be tolerated by the usual means, God supplies the needed coping mechanisms so that we may survive it. For some of His wounded ones, that means is *dissociation.*

Often, for a young child in an extremely abusive environment, dissociation is the only way of escape. God in His wonderful way created us with that ability, giving us this incredible gift when we needed it most.

How does that work? What is dissociation (Dissociative Identity Disorder)? How does this condition occur? What causes it? In this section we'd like to address some of these questions. Following is an article that may shed some light on it.

Dissociative Identity Disorder (DID), formerly known as Multiple Personality Disorder (MPD), is one of the five dissociative disorders identified by the American Psychiatric Association (DSM-IV 1994).

Dissociation occurs when there is a disruption of the normal processes of consciousness, perception, memory, and identity that define a person's individual self. These individuals have the ability to mentally isolate and separate themselves from painful memories and

The Process

traumas they have experienced. While minor forms of dissociation, such as daydreaming, are common and considered normal for all of us to some degree, DID is a severe form of dissociation.

Those with DID tend to compartmentalize their memories, emotions, and coping responses into separate personality states, referred to as alter personalities. Dissociation produces a lack of connection in the individual's thoughts, feelings, memories, and even identity. During a traumatic experience, dissociating from whatever circumstances the person (usually a child) might be in provides a temporary mental escape from the pain of the trauma, which often results in a memory gap, as well (Sidran Foundation 1994). The number of alters within an individual with this disorder often correlates to the severity of the abuse.

Alter personalities may or may not be aware of each other. They may be of different ages, genders, faiths, professions, or even have different IQs, brain waves, or cognitive and physical abilities. Each may hold banks of different memories, have different beliefs, ambitions and outlooks, and present entirely different physical and psychological aspects from the "host" personality (Mayer 1988).

Many of those with DID are able, at least outwardly, to function in a way that few would suspect what is happening within them internally. Most "multiples" are so cut off from their own past memories and emotions that even they are often unable to connect or make sense of their responses and reactions to everyday situations. Often this is because of the dissociative barriers that remain in place, which serve as protective devices from their past experiences. Traumatic memories have been sealed off so that they are unable to invade the consciousness of the person who functions as the presenting personality. Often, however, troubling dreams, depression, anxiety, time loss, and other vague feelings of something not being "right" remain and are a source of distress to the person with DID. These seemingly unrelated "symptoms" are what usually prompts the individual to seek help from a doctor or therapist. Unfortunately, coming to a clear diagnosis can be a long-term and difficult process, but until this occurs, treatment for the underlying symptoms usually proves to be unsuccessful or only provide temporary relief, at best.

What causes such a level of trauma that an individual, a child in particular, would have to go to such extremes as to need to dissociate from all memory of it? According to Psychologist Diane Langberg (1994), it is currently thought that this disorder results from, "severe physical and sexual trauma, accompanied by psychological trauma." She further states that, "DID clients report the highest rates of childhood physical, sexual, and other forms of abuse and trauma among those suffering from any known psychiatric disorder." Most of these victims of abuse describe abuse that was, "profound, relentless, and intolerable," usually occurring before they were five years old, in an environment void of nurturance. Dissociation serves as a protective measure when other sources of protection and safety are not available to the victim of such traumas. Kubetin & Mallory (1992) explain that when a person is, "overwhelmed with severe abuse, torture, or terror, particularly during childhood, the protective mechanism of dissociation may come into play." Combined with certain other environmental conditions, such as repeated early trauma and extreme abuse, the likelihood of dissociation being not only the chosen, but often the only, method of 'escape' from these intolerable conditions becomes even higher.

DID is being identified and studied more than ever before. Researchers who accept "multiplicity" (referring to Multiple Personality Disorder or DID, which is the more modern term describing a child's ability to dissociate and split off) are not entirely agreed on how the syndrome develops, only that early childhood trauma is a factor (Mayer 1988).

Treatment of Dissociative Identity Disorder is a long and difficult process. Those who enter into the process of recovery from the devastating effects of child abuse and severe trauma embark on a challenging journey indeed. The work of healing from the resulting pain and loss is no easy undertaking. Yet there is hope of a positive outcome if disorders such as DID are brought to treatment, and healing truly can take place. It cannot be done alone, however, and

The Process

much help and support is needed for the abuse survivor in order for healing to occur. Dissociative disorders are highly responsive to individual psychotherapy, and the prognosis is good when proper treatment is undertaken and completed.

While some aspects of Dissociative Identity Disorder - not unlike Post Traumatic Stress Disorder - can be controversial in some areas, those suffering from this condition deserve to be heard, to be believed, to be helped, and to be able to receive whatever resources we have available in order for them to reach wholeness and healing.

In the article that follows, Karenjoy explains her own experience with DID which may shed some light on this process and its development:

The Day No Hope Came

I remember the day she came.
"We" were sitting on top of the washing machine in the garage.
Daddy was mad. Again.
And it was all my fault. Again.
Again he had come in my room,
again there was the pain that made me have to not be there in the only way I could,
and again I made a mistake that would result in more hurt, more pain, more shame.
And more fragmentation...

I was already so broken by that time in my life!
already had known pain too well,
had already become too familiar with the rules that only a child living in such circumstances could ever imagine.

I remember that it was daytime still, and he came again anyway.
He was there, and I knew what that meant.

Just Before Dawn

I don't remember any words being spoken, it just wasn't necessary,
because we both knew the drill, but I made the mistake and broke one of the rules -
I flinched.
And that made daddy mad. Again.

So there we were in the garage...he had dragged me out, violently, and threw me
up on the washer.
It was cold -
first, because there was nothing to shield my skin from the cold metal,
but even more than that, because of the fear -
the sheer terror I was feeling
and yet not allowed to show...

He was getting the rope that was hanging on the wall over there in the corner.
And I just knew that it was going to be too much, too hard to take.
I had to go away...

What I knew at that moment was that I couldn't handle it,
I couldn't deal with it, not one more minute, not one more time, not for even one more second.
And so I "left."
Not physically, of course. That wasn't an option.
So I took the only option I had at such times. I "went away" in my mind.
You see, I had a clue at what was about to happen next, and
I was just too tired and worn out, too old and used up to take it any more, too exhausted to withstand the terror I felt.
I was five years old.

Anyway, that's the day No Hope came.
And from that day on she lived inside me and was with me for well over thirty years.

The Process

You see, recounting this incident isn't about shock value, or swapping horror stories. We are not in any way trying to imply, however, that those things don't matter or aren't important. We HAVE to come to the place where we can recognize those things for what they are and not minimize the horrible impact that they have on us. What we are saying, in fact, is that UNLESS we recognize and own these things, neither can we fully recognize and own the healing that is possible when we come to God the Healer with all our brokenness and pain. THAT'S the point of telling this story. That God can take No Hope and can transform it into New Hope and still have all that is or ever will be needed in order to Increase Hope in our lives - not only for those who have suffered the devastating effects of abuse, but for those who will also learn about the Healer as they witness the power of a God for Whom nothing is too hard or impossible. Period.

As with many other survivors of severe abuse, No Hope in Karenjoy's story had companions. Many of them. This is common when the need for survival depends on a well-developed internal system for coping with the unbearable. Perhaps we imagine ourselves right out of the unimaginable. We won't even attempt to explain all the ins and outs of dissociation or go into the details. God knows and understands it completely. We are so thankful for that ability. Like so many others who needed to, many of us used that gift to carry us to the next stage on the journey.

How can we ever sufficiently explain how difficult this is for those who assume that this process is "nothing compared" to the actual abuse itself?

Have you ever been in a car wreck, or helped an accident victim, or been in some other state of emergency that you wondered later how you got through? It seems at the time that we do just what we have to do in order to survive it, to do whatever needs to be done to take care of what we have to take care of. Dealing with the fallout, the consequences, the after-affect, now THAT is hard. So is the process of seeking to find healing from abuse. We should never, never underestimate the incredible cost involved in such an undertaking.

"Rachel" was one survivor's companion whose job was to hold the tears for the others who were not allowed to cry. This is her story.

Rachel's Tears

It seems that I think a lot about Rachel lately.
She was the one who held all the tears.
She never had much to say,
but every now and then you would look around for her
and she was gone.
Sometimes we would wonder where she had gotten to,
but it wasn't hard to figure out.
She had a way of quietly wandering off to be by herself.
We would find her most often in a corner somewhere,
sometimes behind the rocking chair,
or back hiding between the beds on the floor,
or in her secret little hiding place in the closet.
And she would be crying.
Again.
She always looked so little to me,
As if she were sadness itself,
despair embodied,
and so wounded and alone,
so timid and fearful,
so fragile looking.
We never tried to tell her she should stop her tears,
knowing consolations would be empty and pointless.
We all understood the tears
and knew that there were no answers to give her,
so no one tried.
It just was the way things were.
I honor Rachel,
and the many like her,

The Process

*who refuse to let the life springs within them die.
And I will never forget Rachel's tears.*

Perhaps the saddest part about such a story as this one is society's unwillingness to even hear about such things. An experience that brings about the *need* for dissociation in an abused child should never have occurred in the first place. We hear the stories and quickly turn away because of our own discomfort or inability to find a quick fix (which doesn't exist) to make it go away.

A Testimony

by KJ

I was asked to share a testimony at a retreat some time ago. This is what I told them:

"Before I formed you in the womb I knew you; and before you were born I set you apart..." (Jer. 1:5 NIV).

*Before I was born the Lord called me from the womb; from birth He has made mention of my name." "He said to me, you are my servant, in whom I will be glorified"
(Isa. 49:1,3 NIV).*

I chose these verses because they saved my life. The message they conveyed to me was the basis of the stubborn hope that I clung to when life seemed just too intolerable. I'd survived so much! Yet I was terrified that the process of recovery and of taking back all the ground the enemy had stolen from me as a result of my abuse would undo me completely (once and for all!). Too many times, it felt like it almost did, but looking back now, I see how God faithfully kept His promises to me, and I marvel at His patience and strength in bringing me through.

"Thus saith the Lord, In an acceptable time have I heard thee, and in a day of salvation have I helped thee: and I will preserve thee, and give thee for a covenant of the people,
to establish the earth, to cause to inherit the desolate heritages; "That thou mayest say to the prisoners,
Go forth; and to them that are in darkness, Show yourselves!"
(Isa. 49: various KJV).

Looking back now, I can honestly say it was well worth the journey. God did all that He promised, and so much more than I ever dared to hope.

The dictionary says that a testimony is an open declaration, a statement used for evidence or proof. It is also a statement of one's faith by open profession. So I begin my testimony here by stating those things that I know to be absolutely true.

I know that God, the Most High God, Who is my God, is faithful and true. I know that He is not a man that He should lie, but that in Him all truth and only truth dwells. I know that He preserved me and saved me, that He redeemed me and called me, that He rescued and restored me, and that His ongoing work in my life will one day cause me to be presented before His throne wholly complete and changed into His likeness.

These things I know also - that apart from Him my life would be absolutely without hope or meaning or purpose. I know that, in my own eyes, at least, there would be no worth in living, because for as long as I can remember, from my earliest recollection, something that I can only describe as a living death held me in its iron grip, urging me toward destruction in a desperate need for relief. That relief never really came until God began a process of recovery in my life from a very painful past that seems like a whole lifetime ago.

I am a survivor of Satanic Ritual Abuse. Since I lived with my perpetrators, not only did I live with the constant fear of

The Process

what happened at rituals but also what was happening at home on an ongoing basis. I don't remember ever feeling safe, ever. Home was not safe, people were not safe, life was not safe.
I grew up learning that I could depend on absolutely nothing, because dependable things were non-existent in my world, except for one thing: life hurt, and I hurt, beyond description. I knew that. I didn't understand it but I knew it, though not until I was well into my adult years would I even be able to begin to articulate that.

Looking back now I can see that life as I am able to live it now is a marvel. That I am alive is a marvel, and nothing less than proof that the love of God and the power of God are surely the mightiest forces on earth - mightier than the cruelty of man, mightier than the evil intent of the enemy of our souls, mightier than any existing thing in any place.

My journey into healing began with a very simple prayer that went something like this: "God I am so desperate! I don't know what is wrong with me, I don't know why I am like this, and I don't know why I feel so miserable, but I ask You, O God, *please help!*" These were not new words for me, these were not new feelings or emotions, it's just that I had run out of options, run out of places to go to finally try to find some solutions for my inner turmoil and pain. When I least looked for it, God brought me to the place where I would come face to face with what I'd been running from most of all, my past.

Up until that time, I had been walking with the Lord as faithfully as I knew how. I had been involved in Christian ministry in various capacities. I knew, beyond a shadow of doubt, that when I first came to an understanding of Who Christ is, that I had found a good thing, and I never hesitated in receiving His offer of salvation when it was made to me. I was eighteen years old at that time and I was desperate, desperate for a relief from an incredible ache I could not explain. I believed that somehow God had the answers I was seeking, and so I searched. I searched the scriptures, I went to

Just Before Dawn

Bible studies, I listened as people spoke of Him, and I waited for relief to come. And though it is certainly true that God in His infinite capacity to fill that finite hole in a heart that is hungering for Him did do that for me up to a point, I have to confess that something was still very wrong deep inside me, deep where no one else could see (or so I hoped).

There was one particular verse I remember, one that caused me to question every time I read it: II Tim. 4:5, *"make full proof of thy ministry."* I remember writing in the margin of my Bible, "What is my ministry?" It was in the fall of 1991 when I finally began to understand what that was. We had been involved with a lay counseling ministry about that time, and I loved what I was doing, ministering to the needs of God's people in that way. As time went on, God continued to more and more specifically show me who it was I was to minister to: abuse survivors. Somehow, I knew that I knew what these women were feeling and needing, and I felt very privileged to be available to help. I saw God bring help and resolution and relief for them, and even though I didn't know it yet, it was God's way of preparing me for my own journey ahead toward recovery.

It was in the spring of 1992 that I could no longer shut out the old pictures from my own past and had to begin to question their significance; with God's help, I did. I spent the next year working through horrible memories and flashbacks, waking at night from terrifying nightmares, pacing the floor in my living room so no one would see or hear me, cringing in corners with pillows over my mouth so no sound would escape, and I did it, for the most part, alone. It wasn't until June of '93 that I finally called the Freedom in Christ office to get the name of a counselor who could help with issues of satanic ritual abuse. I spent time in counseling working on my own issues before I went back to counseling other survivors of abuse, this time those of SRA only. God had finally shown me just what my ministry was and, more specifically, to whom.

The Process

I spent the next three years trying to walk in the healing God had accomplished in me, and I did that as well as I was able, but some still deeply hidden sorrow continued to nag at me.
I knew that inside was still a well of woundedness and devastation that had never been touched yet, never been healed or restored. I had given God limited access, and had received limited healing. Once again desperation led me into counseling, but this time, to finish the process God began in me years earlier.

What God had taught me through the course of my healing process is that nothing, no memory, no experience, no past abuse, is beyond His ability to heal, to redeem, to restore. There is no depth He cannot plumb or devastation He cannot rebuild and repair. He is the God of possibilities, of light, of life, of hope. That I am living, breathing proof of the love of God is too wonderful for me to fathom. It is my prayer that any who read these words will know the same rich blessing of the Most High God personally and experientially.

Balm for the Hopeless

"Why are you cast down, O my inner self? And why should you moan over and be disquieted within me? Hope in God and wait expectantly for Him; for I shall yet praise Him, Who is the help of my sad countenance, and my God" (Ps. 43:5 Amp).

Each of us have at one time or another experienced the pain that accompanies feelings of hopelessness, and we most likely will again. It is part of the process on our journey to healing. The word of God says to us in Rom. 15:13 that He is the God of hope. God, in His faithfulness, never lets an opportunity pass by to reveal Himself to us more fully and clearly, for He knows it is the best way for us to develop the kind of loving relationship with Him that we wouldn't experience otherwise. It is in those times of hopelessness that we must flee to Him for refuge and reassurance, for restoration of hope

Just Before Dawn

even when all around us in this earthly realm tells us something different.

Hope is all about expectation. The question we must first ask ourselves is, "Where does my expectation lie? On what, or more importantly, upon Whom is my hope set?"

> *"Blessed is he that has the God of Jacob for his help, whose hope is in the Lord his God" (Ps. 146:5). "My soul, wait only upon God, for my expectation is from Him" (Ps. 62:5).*

Expectation here means, hope, the thing that I long for and live for.

The way of beginning to deal with the overwhelming sense of hopelessness that plagues us so cruelly at times is first to identify its source. *"And now, Lord, what wait I for?" (Ps. 39:7).* Really think about this and consider what God may have to say to you. Hopelessness becomes a tool of the enemy when it steals our attention away from Christ, Who is to be the focus of our hopes and expectations, and places it on those temporal things around us. God wants to bring us to the place of saying, *"my hope is in Thee" (Ps. 39:7).* Unless we are quick to come to God, seeking His perspective and truth, the lies and distractions and false perceptions become so seemingly real that it is difficult, to say the least, to differentiate between them and the Truth as it is before God. This leads us into all kinds of trouble, because our natural response is to begin to measure our own strength and abilities to "rise up to the task" and "get ourselves through" instead of putting it into the hands of the Father so that He can. What usually comes next is an even greater sense of hopelessness, as the very thought of having to measure up for one more challenge is just more than we can bear...What a vicious cycle! Thankfully, God has the answer - the solution for every unsolvable puzzle, the provision for every need.

Ephesians 1:17-19 says this: *"I keep asking that the God of our Lord Jesus Christ, the glorious Father, may give you the Spirit of wisdom and revelation, so that you may know Him better. I pray also that the eyes of your heart may be enlightened in order that you may know the*

The Process

hope to which He has called you, the riches of His glorious inheritance in the saints, and His incomparably great power for us who believe." What if, every time we find ourselves faced with feelings of hopelessness, we purposefully use that time as an opportunity to allow God to reveal to us, not only more of His eternal plan and the part we have to play in that, but a greater and clearer vision of Christ Himself? He is the One we can place our hopes upon and not come away ashamed. Never leave God out of the equation or reckon apart from Him. Has He Himself not said that with God nothing shall be impossible? *"God is not a man that He should lie, nor a son of man that He should repent (change His mind): has He said, and shall He not do it? or has He spoken, and shall He not make it good" (Num. 23:19)?* Nothing can change that!

Our hope and prayer for each of us is that we will continue to cling to Christ, however hopeless and impossible the process or situation seems, and that the soothing balm of the Holy Spirit of the Most High God will enter deep within our beings and enable us to rest in hope because of Who He is and all the good that He intends for us, His people.

> *"Now the God of hope fill you with all joy and peace in believing, that ye may abound in hope, through the power of the Holy Spirit" (Rom 15:13).*

He Works

> *He worketh, yea, He worketh still*
> *although at times, these eyes*
> *when set upon these earthly woes,*
> *and my heart within me cries,*
> *I wonder if I've been deceived*
> *or made some grave mistake*
> *in thinking that I knew His will*
> *or had some part to play*
> *in some eternal, sovereign plan*
> *that God was working out...*

*and all at once I'm filled with fear,
or compromise, or doubt...
O help me keep my eyes on Thee!
to stand on what I know,
to walk by faith and not by sight.
Enable me to go
upon the path You choose for me,
with gladness do Your will,
strengthened by this confidence -
He works! He worketh still.*

More on Hope and Perseverance

Diann writes about what she's learned concerning hope in this next article:

"Now hope does not disappoint, because the love of God has been poured out in our hearts by the Holy Spirit Who was given to us" (Rom. 5:5 NKJ).

HOPE - The very word causes a joyful expectation to spring up inside my soul! I happen to be one of those people whose basic personality is a hopeful one. According to the Myers-Briggs Personality Type Indicator, there are four basic personality types: The Practical, The Helpful, The Hopeful, and The Visionary. I fall largely into "The Hopeful" category. Hopeful personality types are intuitive as opposed to sensory. We just *know* within our own souls that things are going to work out. We have hope!

However, in spite of being a hopeful personality type, it is still possible to lose hope due to the hardships of living in a fallen world. Too many trials and too many disappointments can cause even the most optimistic and hopeful person to become disillusioned and lose hope.

So exactly what is it that kills our hope?
The killer is powerlessness. When situations come along that repeatedly show us how very little control we really have in our own affairs of life, we tend to say, "It's hopeless! I can do nothing to change this situation."

Proverbs 13:12 says, "Hope deferred makes the heart sick, but a longing fulfilled is a tree of life." When we lose our hope, we begin to live a dull, boring, monotonous existence. We dig ourselves a rut and climb in, planning to stay there until it's all over.

Have you ever felt the need to kick out both ends of that rut? That desire to "kick" is your hope, trying to rise up and propel you out of the despair and lethargy of hopelessness.

Our past life experiences certainly play a role in our ability to have hope for the future. On the surface, it would seem that if we live largely a trouble-free existence where everything in life comes up roses, we would find it easy to have hope for our future. However, I think the opposite is true. I think that when we have a life filled with trials, sorrows and sufferings, we can still live in hope of a bright future. How? When we have lived through hardships and found that we are still standing, still surviving, we learn the trouble that came upon us did not kill us; we can and should have hope. We find in life that we are able to endure much more than we thought we could. We really don't know what we can endure until we have endured it. Then, looking back, we smile and say, "I don't know how I ever made it through that, but I did." By the grace of God, we keep on surviving, keep on enduring, keep on hoping and finding joy in living.

Hope causes us to press forward, looking into the future with a willingness to risk what we hold onto today for what we *could* have tomorrow. Hope fastens the successes of our past to the anticipation of our future.

Not one of us can know what a day will hold. Yet, we face the new day once again. Do you face it with fear and dread, or do you have an expectant hope for a bright tomorrow?

I think it is safe to say that not every day will be bright and joyful. Some of our days will be difficult and painful. We may temporarily lose our hope. When that happens, bring to mind all those times from your past when God was very present and delivered you from similar circumstances.

He was there all along and He is still present now. He will be present throughout all those days ahead.
Dare to have hope, for the roots of our hopefulness tap into the undercurrent of a river of joy.

"You will show me the path of life; in Your presence is fullness of joy; at Your right hand are pleasures forevermore" (Ps. 16:11).

Running the Race of Grace
By Marilyn

We often speak of a "closet" as being the place where people hide things they don't want others to see or know about. I had such a closet. Twenty-eight years ago, as a new believer, I thought that there were certain things in my life that I didn't want my new Christian friends to know about. So I kept my closet firmly guarded. It was the place where I stuffed my deep wounds, pain, life's disappointments and my feelings.

I put on a happy face, thinking of it as the joy of the Lord, and lived a life of "shoulds and shouldn'ts." Christians shouldn't feel anger or question God about something - if they did, where was their faith? A believer should always be positive in the midst of difficulties, showing their trust and dependence on the Lord alone. Being needy was not an option; I was to be reaching out to others.

The Process

As the years went by, my closet became extremely full of stuffed emotions. It was an unhealthy way to live and eventually my closet door blew off. As a result, I suffered a nervous breakdown and spent a couple of years in dark depression. Praise God that He allowed all that I suffered to bring me to a place of healing and wholeness that was beyond what I ever imagined. I learned that God never intended me to be a lone ranger. Finding my needs met through others did not indicate a lack of trust in Him, rather, I learned how He works through his body, the Church, to meet my needs. I also learned that I needed to risk sharing myself with others so that trust could form, and that I needed to confess to others so that I might be healed. I don't need to be vulnerable with everyone but I do need at least a couple of friends I can be totally honest with-who will encourage me and confront me as needed.

This is just a touch of all that God is teaching me about living in a healthy manner. I'm on a journey. The Bible refers to it as sanctification; Paul calls it the race. Sanctification is not something that just happens; it must be pursued relentlessly. 1 Thessalonians talks about being sanctified wholly in body, soul, and spirit. My emotions are real and need to be expressed - but God never intended me to be ruled by them. It is in my mind that spiritual battles are fought - so I need to learn about the lies I tell myself and change inwardly by telling myself the truth. Instead, with my will I either decide to follow Christ or I decide to continue in patterns that are damaging to myself and others.

Surely the most wonderful blessing in opening a closet is that once the pain, confusion and ugliness are cleaned out, God can then fill it with His true peace and joy. I've had to wrestle with the deep things of God: why did He allow me to be so victimized and wounded? There were times that I deeply longed for an intimate relationship with my Father and Redeemer, but couldn't quite bring myself to trust Him fully. There are no easy answers but I believe that when we are honest with God, He will bring peace to the confusion. He did that for me and it has opened up a new dimension and depth in my relationship with Him.

God is good all of the time, even when I can't understand the work He's doing in me. People can misunderstand the process of recovery and wonder why it is important to look at something that happened years ago. When we allow ourselves to feel our emotions and process them when they occur, then the healing begins to take place. However, if we ignore painful situations when they happen, we can obstruct healing. The situation remains unprocessed and doesn't disappear- it ends showing up in current behavior. Once a person goes back and processes the original feeling, a connection can be made to present behavior. The behavior may be recognized as a way to deaden the pain from the past or a way to protect oneself from further hurt. When the original wound is uncovered, the great Healer can free a person from the awful cycle of addiction or repetitive unhealthy behavior.

Diann writes the following:

The recovery journey is a long one and the movement from woundedness to wholeness is a life-long undertaking. Adults who were sexually abused in their childhood have many obstacles to overcome. Abuse victims struggle with many issues; one of the most complex issues to face is the interwoven role of shame and contempt. Recently, I've been discovering some important truths about the function of contempt in my life. I knew I had felt a deep sense of shame for decades, but could never seem to put my finger on its exact cause. As I struggled with my understanding, the Holy Spirit was hard at work in me, exposing the lies that the abuse taught me about God, others and myself. When I got down to the inner part of my soul, into the "who I am" core of my being, I was shocked to find that I had a deep-seated view of myself as a "whore." That was surprising to me because on one level of my understanding, I knew that was not the truth. I was victimized as a child and knew that I had been helpless and quite powerless to change those events in my life. The real truth, which was deeply buried within my soul, hit me like a lightning bolt. Most abuse survivors will struggle with shame and contempt at some point in their recovery journey. One of the books I read deals in-depth with the aspects of shame. The book, *The Wounded Heart* by Dr. Dan B. Allender, is one I've read about five times now and I am also working my way through the accompanying workbook. It is an in-depth study of how sexual abuse affects the human psyche and exposes the roots of the damage to the human soul and spirit. It is a book and workbook that is well worth the investment of both money and time. It has helped me to plow up the rock-hard ground of my heart by going back over the soul-soil time and time again, breaking up more and more of the large clumps of dirt and rocks, while also plucking out more and more of the weeds that have grown in the field of my heart as a result of my abusive past.

Because my abuse was at the hands of my own parents, it was soul shattering to me, both as a child and as an adult. Parents are supposed to love and care for their children, not abuse and misuse them. So, instead of facing the truth about my own parents, I simply shoved that truth aside and rewrote my own story. In my mind, I created parents who were more loving and caring, who had my best interest at heart. Then I accepted this story as the truth of my life. In order to do that, I had, in the deepest level of my being, to believe that the abuse was somehow my fault. I was the one who was sinful and vile. The image of the prostitute or whore became the core image of my being. That image was buried very deeply and was covered over by a very pleasant, although extremely deadened, personality. No one could ever be allowed to deeply know me or to touch the inmost core of who I am, for that core was dirty, vile, and shameful. The self-contempt in my life was huge. I saw myself as flawed, incompetent and inferior. I would constantly beat myself up over every perceived sin or wrong that I committed. As a Christian believer, I repented repeatedly for my every sin. It was as if the blood of Jesus could never wash me clean; I was too dirty to ever be clean. On the surface, I was a born-again Christian believer, but the blood had never reached the inmost parts of my being. The discovery of these truths about myself and about my God were soul changing. The process began with my own repentance. Not for the perceived sin of being sexually abused (which was never my sin) but for the sin of creating a false reality instead of believing the truth about my own world and my own parents. From my earliest childhood and on into my adulthood, I chose to believe the lie and escape the painful reality of my life. As an adult, I have come to see that a change in my perception is needed; seeing myself as God sees me (and always has seen me), and allowing myself to see my parents and the home I came from in a truthful fashion, even though that truth is still very painful to me. No one likes pain, but pain will not kill us; we must learn to embrace the pain in order to be free from it.

The Wounded Heart Workbook beautifully describes the role of self-contempt: "First, by blaming myself I was able to view my family as happy and healthy and to deny the overwhelming sadness, aloneness, and emptiness that was present in my home. Second, as long as I remained the problem, there was hope that there was something I could do to make my life happier, it insulated me from having to admit my dependency upon Christ." Most of us desperately want to find a way to make our lives work. However, our mistake is in trying to make life work apart from God. There are two types of contempt at work within our wounded souls, other-centered contempt and self-centered contempt. Again, quoting from the workbook, "Other-centered contempt ignores one's own depravity ("for all have sinned and fallen short of the glory of God.") and centers the blame on another person's failure. It is Satan's counterfeit for loving rebuke. Other-centered contempt involves analysis for the aim of exploitation, feedback for the purpose of control. Self-contempt is Satan's counterfeit for conviction over sin. We've been hurt, terribly hurt. In our fallenness, our desires for love, intimacy, respect, attention, security, and a dozen others have become demands that we, others, and God give us what we want. When we, others, and God fail to grant or even hear those desires/demands, fierce rage begins to erupt in the deep places of our souls. It often never reaches the surface as volcanic violence and heat. Instead, it bubbles up and hardens as ice-cold rock that covers our hearts. Have our demands been rejected? Very well, we will reject our rejecters: self, others and God. I will not hurt! We vow, *I will create for myself a better world, a better self, a better God!* The pronouncements of contempt may be shouted with fury, muttered cynically, or accompanied by a pleasant smile."

It takes time to see clearly exactly how we are damaged and how we responded to that damage. The truths I found here have helped me to gain more healing and more freedom and a closer relationship with my God as He continues to pour His love into my wounded heart.

Today, I am able to see clearly the failures of my parents and the damage to my soul. I also see clearly that I belong to a loving and benevolent God who sees and understands it all. Not only does He see and understand, He is able to touch and heal the soul wounds of sexual abuse. The wall of shame and contempt can be removed. Once again, repentance and forgiveness come into play. Forgiveness is a process; it can never be just a one-time event, but must become a way of life. Once I was able to see my family as they really are, I was able to forgive their failures. As long as we live in denial and deception, we will not see the need to forgive. Once the eyes of our understanding are open, we can begin the long process of forgiveness as we take down the walls of shame and contempt through broken-hearted repentance of our inappropriate responses to the abuse. God's desire is for us to exchange the lies that the abuse taught us for the truth of His word.

Just Before Dawn

> *"And you shall know the truth, and the truth shall make you free" (John 8:32).*

Out of the Depths

I asked myself once, a long time ago, if perhaps there was, after all, a pit too deep for the arm of God to reach down into and save from. I wondered if, just maybe, there could be a level of darkness too impenetrable for God to see through. I feared that there just possibly could be damage too devastating and beyond repair for even Him to be able to heal. I was afraid that such a life as the one I had lived and barely survived might be beyond His ability or willingness to redeem.

However, as He always is, God was up to the challenge. He proved to me that even the horrors of ritual abuse were not too much for Him to recover me from and that the despair and desolation left upon my soul by my abusers was not too great a task for Him to bring restoration and renewal to.

It was not too long after beginning to recover memories of my childhood abuse that this poem came to me as a result of a decision to go on the healing journey, one that I realized even then would be a long and difficult process. Hard and painful as it was at times, God was true to His word and set the captive free at last from long years of bondage and grief. It was there in the deep and dark places I found Him most brilliantly radiant, and in the depths of hopeless despair that He lifted me to realms of peace and purpose.

> *Out of the depths He rescues me,*
> *Unbinds my fetters, makes me free,*
> *Redeems my life, restores my hope,*
> *Equips, enables me to cope,*
> *Gives me reason to exist,*
> *Invites me to His aid enlist,*
> *Sheds His light for battles dark,*
> *Provides the courage to embark*

The Process

> *on journeys I would never go*
> *but for His strength, to face the foe,*
> *Unfurls my banner on the field,*
> *Routs the enemy, makes him yield*
> *to His authority, power, and might,*
> *Reclaims the ground, rekindles light!*
>
> *Dare I give way to fear and doubt?*
> *Forget His mercy? Turn about?*
> *Retreat in shame? Reject His aid?*
> *Refuse His love? Through the mire wade?*
>
> *Nay! I must to the fountain fly,*
> *Forsaking sin, myself deny,*
> *Must run to His voice obey,*
> *Fight the fight, await the day,*
> *Then must to His prompting heed,*
> *For His people intercede,*
> *His joy my strength, His grace my song,*
> *My confidence - I to Christ belong!*

I'm glad I didn't quit, that I didn't give in to the voices that insisted I halt because of my fears and inability to endure on my own.

As the hart pants after the water brooks, so pants my soul after Thee, O God. My soul thirsts for God, for the living God: when shall I come and appear before God? My tears have been my meat day and night, while they continually say unto me, Where is thy God? O my God, my soul is cast down within me. I will say unto God my rock, Why have You forgotten me? Why go I mourning because of the oppression of the enemy? As with a sword in my bones, my enemies reproach me; while they say daily to me, Where is thy God? Why art thou cast down, O my soul? and why art thou disquieted within me? Hope thou in God; for I shall yet praise Him, Who is the health of my countenance, and my God! The Lord will command His loving

kindness in the daytime, and in the night His song shall be with me"
(Ps. 42 various).

Just Before Dawn

In the darkened hours of my soul's nighttime I sought Him,
groping blindly from place to place.
I yearned for the warmth of the living God
and prayed for a refuge of safety from the shadowed specters that seemed to follow me wherever I went.
I despaired at the inky blackness that enfolded me like a shroud,
for my eyes could not pierce it, however intently I set my gaze to discover some Source of Light in it.
Through the long night I stumbled on, tripping at every bump in my path
and fearing a death fall over some unseen precipice,
startling at every sound, so magnified by my fears.
I thought I had journeyed like this forever!
and wondered, would I ever make it through?
It was just before dawn…

*Just before dawn it's darkest,
and the nighttime seems most cold,
and the world all about feels so friendless,
but there, though doubting, I'm told
that then is when stars shine brightest,
and if I but look up I'd see
the heavens declaring God's glory
and faithful promise to me
that though I fear, or grow weary,
no matter how deep my despair,
as surely as day follows nighttime,
God has always been here,*

The Process

> *His arms open wide to receive me*
> *whenever to him I should flee,*
> *and though I can't see much now clearly,*
> *He's here within reach beside me.*
> *Oh, help me to rest in assurance*
> *that Light once again will prevail,*
> *and scatter the darkness far from me.*
> *remind me how You cannot fail…*
>
> *Now I hear them! The songs of the night birds,*
> *and all at once I am drawn*
> *to sing with them, Day Light is coming!*
> *this dark hour's the one before dawn.*

The Process can be a long and difficult one, and making the decision to commit to seeing it through can be a terrifying one, but however dark and difficult the path ahead, God is up to the challenge, and is more than able to see us through to restoration. The realization of our greatest hope could be just around the next bend! Whatever it is that would hinder us from getting there must be left behind with any other thing that would keep us from all that God has promised those who would follow Him.

<u>Helps</u>

"From where does my help come?" Psalm 121:1

It was another one of those days - a day when I wondered where I would get the strength to hold on just one more time. I began to look around me. *I'm so weary, Lord. I just can't do it.* Dishes, laundry, a checkbook to balance, work to attend to, then the sound of my daughter in the next room...*I'll do it for her, for my sons and my husband. How could he ever take care of them alone?* But I had said that the last time I was in this place, the last time I felt overwhelmed and frustrated and like I could barely make it through. *Now look at me; again, I'm just not there for them. Again I'm unable to get myself up and do what I should; again never quite able to measure up, always feeling like a failure, defeated and sad and oh so tired...*And once again, I asked myself, *Why? Wouldn't they all be better off without me??*

There were other times, too, that brought me far too close to the breaking point; times when such deep disappointment came, either in myself and the overwhelming feelings of shame and guilt I had as a mother (or wife, or friend, or "good" Christian, *or whatever*), times when the misunderstandings and rejection I felt as my family and friends who just could not understand the pain and costliness of the healing process seemed beyond my ability to bear. How could they? At such times those feelings of wondering if they honestly would be better off without me were so intense and difficult to get through. I couldn't help but wonder if it was worth it all.

That was quite a while ago, and thankfully, I did hold on, and I did get through, but not until I came to the place first where I began to measure things from an entirely different perspective. The conclusion I finally had to come to was that if my health or healing or sense of worth and value had to be dependent upon my own resources, or upon any other person, then disappointment and discouragement were sure to follow. It is unfair to put that kind of burden for performance either upon myself or on those I love or hope will help meet my needs and expectations. Only God can fill the place of God, and until I really began to understand and believe the truth that His love and acceptance were absolutely unconditional because they were unchangeable and based on *His Son's work* in me did I begin to come to the place of hope and peace. Much of the instability and despair left me, and as a result I really was able to "be there" more than I had before, not only for my children and others outside but also for my own internal processes taking place within me. I finally began to enter into the rest He promises as the pressure of having to "be" or perform in order to be accepted *or acceptable* eased from off of my weary shoulders. What a relief! This can be such a slow and difficult place to come to for so many of us, but it is a message that those of us who are afraid to believe the good, who are afraid to trust, who are afraid to hope, must be reminded of again and again.

Those who must live with the devastating effects of abuse can certainly relate to the cruel lies our perpetrators taught us; that we are responsible for having to do it perfectly, that we must do it alone, that we are entirely worthless unless we do it "right" and measure up to all the demands. The truth is that our lives are not pointless and without value, no matter what stage of the journey we are on! Our abusers may have forced us to keep silent, but silence is the very thing that steals our life away from us and robs us of our personhood. It causes us to live in that isolated vacuum they put us in where despair can overwhelm us.

My prayer is that somehow, some way, the forces of darkness will be held back by the shining light of God's truth as we share it with one another AND are allowed to speak out our struggles and fears with those who are safe and willing to hear. We cannot do it alone! The good news is that God never intended us to. We <u>can</u> break free from the despair that weighs us down, we can make a difference for good, we can heal, and we can do more than just hold on from one crushing moment to the next.

"From the end of the earth I will cry to You, When my heart is overwhelmed, Lead me to the rock that is higher than I." Psalm 61:2

Some Practical Tools

So what *does* help? How do we get from here to there? And what about all that space in between? We'd like to offer some practical tools for you to use right now, things to think about and look for, so that you can get to the other side with as much assistance and encouragement as one traveler on the journey can offer another. We've listed some things that we found we needed to help make the path more travel-able.

Become informed. Learn about the stages of recovery that are common for those seeking to heal from the after-affects of abuse. Find a safe, well-informed counselor who can assist you in your healing process and help equip you with the tools you need in order to heal. This can be an incredibly empowering thing in itself.

There are some wonderful resources out there. *The Wounded Heart* by Dan Allender is a good one at whatever stage of the sexual abuse healing journey you are on. Read the good material (we'll provide a list of a few of those resources at the back of the book for you) on the subject of healing from abuse that is available. Attend a safe, supportive group or Bible study so that you have the encouragement and accountability of others on the healing path. When we know what the challenges are before us we can often be better prepared to meet them.

Dissociative disorders for example, can present a whole unique set of challenges for those whose only defense was to "go away" while their abuse was occurring. Dissociation is not the same as repression

Helps

(which occurs *after* a traumatic event). It occurs *while* an overwhelming event is happening and is one way to "forget" the trauma, at least temporarily. For many, dissociating helped us function normally by helping us to block out the memory of the traumatic circumstances we lived with. If you are seeking counseling for help in this area, be sure your counselor has a working knowledge of dissociative disorders.

A Brief Overview of DID is in the last section *(The Process)* under Coping Mechanisms. For a more complete discussion see Dr. James Friesen's book, *Uncovering the Mystery of MPD*, which is full of information on how MPD (now called DID) works. Additionally, the Sidran Foundation has an online site that offers helpful and informative articles on the topics of DID and PTSD for both survivors and support people. You may also visit my website on DID which has additional links and information at http://www.suite101.com/welcome.cfm/DID

Post Traumatic Stress Disorder is another condition that can result from trauma. This disorder is not uncommon in those suffering with DID. The flashbacks and nightmares can often become so disabling that we must seek extra help and support in dealing with it. It is not an issue of weakness, but of necessity. Being informed as to what is common in dealing with these issues brings a sense of relief, especially from the condemnation too many of us feel at not being able to "measure up" to what is supposedly "normal," whatever that is!

Post Traumatic Stress Disorder, or PTSD, is an acquired (reactive) disorder that results from exposure to extreme trauma, "an event outside normal human experience" that leaves the one experiencing it feeling powerless, helpless, paralyzed, and yet forced to focus consciousness in attempts to cope. PTSD was officially recognized as a psychological disorder in 1980 when a great number of war veterans were displaying the after-affects of their wartime experiences. It was once thought that when a conflict ended and danger was past that the symptoms of having been involved in an extreme or life-threatening

Just Before Dawn

trauma would naturally abate with the passing of time. In recent years, however, the medical and psychological communities have begun to realize that the psychological and emotional damage these experiences can cause do not heal so naturally as was earlier assumed or hoped.

War veterans were not the only ones exhibiting the signs of PTSD. Many survivors of other types of traumas or terrifying ordeals, such as victims of rape, violent assaults, childhood abuse, and/or those who had witnessed any event where an experience of terror or threat (or perceived threat) to "life or limb," also displayed the same kinds of symptoms. Recent studies have revealed that one group, in particular, has been shown to be at extreme risk for developing this condition: Victims of childhood sexual abuse face the greatest risk of developing Post Traumatic Stress Disorder.

Individuals who have been abused as children, especially when the nature of the abuse is sexual and/or physical in nature, are highly prone to a chronic form of this disorder. Studies of abused children support this, particularly in cases where the abuse is physical and/or sexual (Widom, 1223-1229, 1999). Many people still only equate combat trauma, once called shell shock or battle fatigue, with PTSD but some experiences such as rape and repeated or severe abuse are even more likely to produce symptoms of post traumatic stress in individuals (Sidran Foundation, 1-3, 2001). According to the Associate Professor of the School of Social Work at the University of Southern California, Ferol Mennen, "Child abuse has increasingly been recognized as a serious life trauma and a potential trigger for Post Traumatic Stress Disorder and PTSD-symptoms" (In Press).

Symptoms can include psychological problems, such as depression and anxiety, or physical problems, such as chronic pain and other ailments that seem to have no other explanation. Self-destructive behaviors are also common, including alcohol and drug abuse. According to the Diagnostic and Statistical Manual of Mental Disorders, some of the specific symptoms of PTSD can include recurrent and intrusive flashbacks of the event(s), nightmares, intense psychological distress, persistent avoidance of related stimuli, hypervigilance, extreme startle response, and dissociative disorders (468).

Many children who have been abused in these ways may not display the signs of posttraumatic stress until long after the abuse has ceased (Sidran, 1995-2000). Most often the symptoms do not become obvious enough to be recognized and then treated until well into the adult years. Often a victim of repeated abuse develops a form of coping, called dissociation, in order to block out the traumatic experience from their conscious mind. Throughout their lives, abuse survivors will attempt to dissociate from or avoid situations that remind them of their traumatic experiences, thereby delaying recall of the events. Bessel van der Kolk (2001), one of the foremost authorities on traumatic memory, has noted that "many cognitive scientists [take] an incredulous stance" (10) on this issue, denying its validity, arguing that because of lack of empirical evidence retrieved traumatic memories could be inaccurate. He points out, however, that not being able to observe this process of delayed recall in a laboratory setting does not justify the stance that retrieved traumatic memories are unreliable (11-12). Forgetting, and then later recovering, traumatic memories has, in fact, been well documented over the years. Freyd (1998), an academic psychologist and an abuse survivor who experienced delayed recall of her own abuse, asserts in her letter to the editor of the Register-Guard that there has been an explosion of empirical research in this area, especially research on memory for childhood sexual abuse (12A).

Individuals with a history of childhood sexual abuse (CSA) most often develop this disorder as a result of their extreme need to find some way to cope with ongoing trauma, leading to chronic PTSD. Van der Kolk (1996) stresses that "dissociation that occurs at the time the trauma appears to be the single most important predictor for the establishment of chronic PTSD" (66). He further asserts that the connection between CSA and the emergence of these disorders "has become increasingly clear" (66). Because children are easily overwhelmed by the feelings of helplessness, powerlessness, and the inability to escape what would be for anyone intolerable circumstances, "forgetting" the trauma by dissociating from it is a much more common coping mechanism than once was originally thought. According to Hopper (2001), "Amnesia for childhood sexual abuse is a condition. The existence of this condition is beyond dispute." In conclusion, though the study of PTSD can at times be a controversial subject, there is sufficient evidence to support the position that individuals who have experienced childhood sexual abuse are among the highest population of traumatic experience victims to develop Post Traumatic Stress disorder. Furthermore, studies to date have shown that those who would argue this issue cannot deny the mounting evidence that delayed recall in the development Post Traumatic Stress Disorder is more common than once was believed. PTSD is often the result of coping and surviving such a trauma.

Depression is yet another issue common to survivors of abuse. Depression is more than having just a blue day or feeling occasional sadness. We must know the difference between dysthymia (despondency in mood) and clinical depression. Major Depressive Disorder is a serious condition that needs to be recognized and treated.

For those who have suffered with such a condition for long periods of time, it may not be easily recognized. Bouts may come on without notice.

One survivor in the midst of a severe depressive episode wrote the following in her journal during one such episode. One caution here first, however. Beware of the natural tendency to compare, even when it is unrealistic to do so. While those who share similar backgrounds can certainly relate on some level, each of us are unique and may manifest symptoms of depression in different ways. Not everyone experiences depression in this particular manner, nor does depression have to lead to such depth of despair, though it can. Depression is treatable, and when it is addressed, it is curable. What we must not do is deny or minimize depression, either. "Well, I'm not

Helps

that bad, therefore I don't have a problem and I don't have to deal with it," is not the stance to take if it is interfering with one's level of functioning. Occasional depression is a normal part of the healing process, but it should also be temporary.

Into the Abyss - Diary of Depression
By Robyn

Day One

Deep into the mouth of madness I go. I never know when it will happen, what will set it off. Each time I am taken by surprise as I trip over the giant teeth of my depression, teeth that rip and shred my psyche. Down I go, slipping on the evil tongue that voices hurtful words from my childhood, screaming prophecies that I pray are not true. As it swallows me, I fall into the nothingness of my personal agony. I fear that my fate is sealed, sealed by the tears of my youth. I fear never being able to recover. I long for the silence of death, the release of my soul into nothingness, blessed. Does anyone know? NO! Should I share it? Would it help? More than likely it would only make people run from me. I don't think they would feel my pain, I don't think it would help.

Day Two

Two days: my descent into hell has only been two days. It seems like a lifetime, like it has always been and always will be. I'm scared and I'm tired. Very, very tired. Empty. The well has run dry. I can no longer think or feel. Nothing comes to mind but the desire for an end. Please, no more, no more life. I'm much too weak to take it. I've failed. I'm not good enough to withstand the storm.

Day Three

I'm beginning to feel better. Thank God for my friends. My friends talk and listen. Even if they don't understand they don't pin a label on me. They feel much more for me than

Just Before Dawn

anyone in my family. Family members tell me I have so much to live for. Sure. Right. I sense that they don't want to lose a target. It's my family who has put me here, clinging to the edge of the pit. It is up to me to get away from them, putting a healing distance between us. I have to talk. To not talk is to die and my family has been killing me little by little all my life. Family secrets abound, so many that I can't remember the ones I know. I wonder how many I don't know? The horrors I do remember are enough to make me shiver. Even though I dread knowing those truths, I ache to find them.

Day Four

I can breathe. I can finally take a deep breath and know that even though I'm not through the storm I will make it. I can look up and not feel as if the world is on my chest. I know that I will emerge battered but not beaten.

After Thoughts

I wonder why I didn't kill myself that first day. I was so very close. My mind called for the release of pain, the bliss of not feeling. What stopped me? I prayed and asked God if He would really banish me to the Biblical Hell I was taught about in my childhood. My hell, I thought, was here on earth. My idea of Heaven is peace. How ironic it would be to seek release and end up in an eternity of pain and sorrow. *The answer for now is both faith and fear.*

Suicidal thoughts *can accompany depression.* What *will* stop us? How will we find the strength to hold on until the healing can come? *As long as there is life there is hope!* How do we hold on to that belief rather than the one that says there is no hope? What if our faith is not strong enough to get us through, then what? Hope deferred, after all, does make the heartsick. *Sometimes the only answer is to stop the struggle by allowing others to carry us to Jesus when we cannot get there ourselves.* Like the account of the paralyzed man on the cot whose friends carried him and lowered him through a hole in

Helps

the roof to get him to the feet of Jesus, so must those who have the strength carry those who do not at such times. Christ meant His body of believers to hold each other up in this way; He did not intend for us to do it entirely on our own. Our part is simply, if we are the ones who cannot walk, to allow others who can to come alongside and by *their* faith carry us to the Healer so that we can continue on to the next stage on the journey.

What is God's perspective on depression? Let's look at one example of a man who became deeply depressed, Elijah.

This story starts back in I Kings 17. Elijah was a prophet of God with some (not only) pretty impressive credentials (his name meant, "Yahweh is God") but connections in high places, as well. He apparently had everything going for him. He had clout (I Kings 17:1 he had audience and access to king himself), he had spiritual standing and authority, too (how many people were walking around saying things like, "the Lord God of Israel...before Whom I stand..." He had the words of authority ("there shall be...according to my words,"). He had the God of Creation Himself looking after him and providing for him (I Kings 17:4 "And it shall be, that thou shalt drink of the brook, and I have commanded the ravens to feed thee there"). He had a confidence in himself that few of us know (I Kings 17:13 "make me a cake first...") based on personal knowledge and experience with his God. He had (apparently) more gifts than most of us could ever even begin to imagine - ability to heal (17:22), power over the weather (18:1), power over the air (18:2), power over the forces of nature (18:38, 41). He even had power over those 400 priests of Baal (18:40). This guy even outran a chariot (18:46), and all that in just two chapters!!

I wonder, however, if Elijah began to get caught up in the same trap many of us do; he began to incorporate into his belief system those things he saw and experienced in the physical realm and drew some of *his own* conclusions. He sought to "work it out" in his own strength, and it had a huge impact on him. Perhaps he began to feel that he was more responsible than he really was to do something based on that assumption? Perhaps he thought that whatever God

Just Before Dawn

wanted to accomplish through him was more dependent upon *him* than it really was?

What is the key to knowing we're falling into that trap? I Kings 18:22 *"I, even I only..."* He began to believe that he was alone and unique, that he was having to take the whole mess upon himself...and he became overwhelmed, he became angry and discouraged, he became impatient and resentful, maybe he even became a little prideful, and then he began to make judgments and decisions based on that belief.

No wonder Elijah got depressed!

Here's the scenario: I Kings 19:1-21 tells us, *"Now Ahab told Jezebel everything Elijah had done and how he had killed all the prophets with the sword.*

"So Jezebel sent a messenger to Elijah to say, May the gods deal with me, be it ever so severely, if by this time tomorrow I do not make your life like that of one of them."

Verse 3 tells us that Elijah was afraid and ran for his life. You would think that a man with such gifts, such fellowship with the God Who gave them, would demonstrate a little more faith and courage when it came to Jezebel's threats! But, based on some faulty beliefs that had developed somewhere along the line, Elijah made certain choices, and as a result bore some pretty painful and difficult consequences.

"When he came to Beersheba in Judah, he left his servant there." Big mistake! He isolated. Isolation cuts us off from the very resources God has provided for those times in our lives when we get tired and overwhelmed and just plain weary, which we all do and will again (and maybe again) at one time or another.

"[W]hile he himself went a day's journey into the desert." That was an interesting choice of locations. Maybe it was the best place that described or represented the dryness and desolation he was feeling at the time. Maybe it was the only place he could get alone. The good

Helps

news about the desert is that even in the desert God is there. Where it feels lifeless and lonely and growth seems so stunted and colorless, God is still there.

"He came to a broom tree, sat down under it, and prayed that he might die." Now that's depression!

"I have had enough, LORD," he said. I'm tired. I'm sick and tired. I've had it.

"Take my life; I am no better than my ancestors." I wonder to what or to whom he was comparing himself? What standard (or whose) was he measuring himself by? My question at this point is, Elijah, who told you that you had to be?! When and where and at what point did that become an issue? And what does that have to do with your service for God? How does that change God's character or ability to be God in you and for you??

"Then he lay down under the tree and fell asleep." (Another sign of depression, of course.)

"All at once an angel touched him and said, 'Get up and eat.'" I love the way God comes to us, the way He reaches out to us again and again, even when we're not always able to reach back.

"He looked around." Maybe he hadn't forgotten everything at that point. At least he looked, remembering, perhaps, that when God speaks we can expect something to happen.

"[A]nd there by his head was a cake of bread baked over hot coals, and a jar of water. He ate and drank and then lay down again." I think that was totally okay with God. He knew where Elijah was and how he was feeling. He knew he was exhausted, and it really was okay for him to just rest at that point.

"The angel of the LORD came back a second time and touched him (again)." God is persistent, thankfully. His refusal to give up on us is so incredible. Isaiah 30:18 says that the Lord waits to be gracious

Just Before Dawn

to us. That's such good news to some of us who are slow learner-responders!

"[A]nd said, 'Get up and eat, for the journey is too much for you.'"
I used to think this was a judgment, a rejection of sorts, or that it meant a disqualification for the work, but I don't believe that anymore. Our God is a Redeemer! His way is all about restoration, and His character is compassionate. God understood that Elijah was tired. He understood that he needed an encounter with the living God in a way he had perhaps missed (or maybe was forgetting) in all his activity and work for God. *Come aside, Elijah. Right now I don't want you to work, I don't want you to prophesy, I don't want you to perform, I don't want you to do great miracles or incredible deeds. All I want you to do is rest, and let Me minister to you. Come and meet Me at Horeb, the mount of God where Moses before you stood and met with Me, because I have something awesome I want to show you!* That's God.

"So he got up and ate and drank. Strengthened by that food, he traveled forty days and forty nights until he reached Horeb, the mountain of God." When we eat at God's table, something amazing happens.

"There he went into a cave and spent the night." The King James Version says he *lodged* there. That word means, o*bstinate, grudge.* Elijah was still angry.

"And the word of the LORD came to him." God spoke. He began the slow process of helping Elijah come to terms with the issues that were on his heart.

"What are you doing here, Elijah?" Tell Me what's happened. Tell Me your concerns. I'm listening…But Elijah, search your own heart.

He replied, *"I have been very zealous for the LORD God Almighty. The Israelites have rejected your covenant, broken down your altars, and put your prophets to death with the sword. I am the only one left, and now they are trying to kill me too."*

Helps

So God responded, not with a rebuke, not with a lecture, but with a demonstration…

"The LORD said, Go out and stand on the mountain in the presence of the LORD, for the LORD is about to pass by." I want to show you something, Elijah, and I don't want you to miss it!

"Then a great and powerful wind tore the mountains apart and shattered the rocks before the LORD, but the LORD was not in the wind." When I looked up that word for wind, *Strong's Exhaustive Concordance* said that it literally meant, *a violent exhalation, anger.* Note that God was not in the wind!

"After the wind there was an earthquake, but the LORD was not in the earthquake." Earthquake meant, *uproar, confused noise, fierceness.* God was not there either!

"After the earthquake came a fire, but the LORD was not in the fire." Is there anything more devastating and destructive than a fire? It only leaves ashes. But there is no burning, no destruction in Him. The Spirit of God, rather, brings refreshment and life. That is the Truth.

"And after the fire came a gentle whisper." King James says, *"A still small voice."* Literally, *a sound of gentle stillness. Quiet, calm. A gentle bleating (Strong's).* Matthew Henry comments, *"God speaks in whispers soft, not in those dreadful sounds!"*

"When Elijah heard it, he pulled his cloak over his face." Some suggest this was a sign of humility, because he knew that God was addressing him. Others say it was shame that caused him to cover his face. I don't know, but whatever compelled him to do that, it's obvious that Elijah recognized that he was walking out into the presence of God, and he met with Him there.

"[A]nd went out and stood at the mouth of the cave." (I wonder if all that fearful racket drove him there inside?)

Just Before Dawn

"Then a voice said to him, 'What are you doing here, Elijah?'"
Ah, the persistence and tenacity of God again! An opportunity for re-evaluation. After what you've seen today, Elijah, tell Me, why are you still here?

Verse 14: *"He replied, I have been very zealous for the LORD God Almighty. The Israelites have rejected your covenant, broken down your altars, and put your prophets to death with the sword. I am the only one left, and now they are trying to kill me too."* In other words, Elijah must have been feeling, I'm still concerned about all this <u>stuff</u>! And I'm still overwhelmed by the enormity of it all! (No wonder!)

"The LORD said to him, Go back the way you came." Let's retrace a bit here, Elijah. I know you didn't like it back there, but you've had some time off with Me for a while, and I've shown you a thing or two. You're better equipped now. And I'm not done over there yet! So, here's the plan - you know, the rest of the plan you didn't know about...Let's retrace some of those steps together a bit.

"[G]o to the Desert of Damascus. When you get there, anoint Hazael king over Aram." Now Hazael was a warlike kind of guy. He liked a good fight. He, in fact, later took the Syrian throne, which weakened Ahab's position. This was part of God's plan to bring correction for the idolatry in the land (addressing Elijah's concerns).

"Also, anoint Jehu son of Nimshi king over Israel." Jehu was a known Baal opponent. He seized the throne from Ahab and wiped out Ahab's house. He cleaned house for God.

"[A]nd anoint Elisha son of Shaphat from Abel Meholah to succeed you as prophet." In other words, I'm going to raise up someone to help you, Elijah, someone to minister to you and to lighten your load and support you. This guy is young and energetic and vigorous and whole-hearted (whew!) and he will do a great job of carrying on your work. (Not only that, and Elijah didn't know it then, but Elisha later saw to the destruction of the children of Bethel - the adherents of Baal) Rest assured! Your God has got it all under control!

Helps

"Jehu will put to death any who escape the sword of Hazael, and Elisha will put to death any who escape the sword of Jehu." Not only do I have a plan, but I've got back ups!

Verse 18*: "Yet I reserve seven thousand in Israel—all whose knees have not bowed down to Baal and all whose mouths have not kissed him."* God will never lack instruments to see to His will being accomplished.

"So Elijah went from there and found Elisha son of Shaphat. He was plowing with twelve yoke of oxen, and he himself was driving the twelfth pair." Ah, a hard worker at last! A man who's not above getting his hands dirty, a man willing to get in there and go for it!

"Elijah went up to him and threw his cloak around him." (The invitation.)

Elisha then left his oxen and ran after Elijah. (The response.)

"Let me kiss my father and mother good-by, he said, and then I will come with you." Hmm…Devoted, considerate, respectful…

"Go back," Elijah replied. (The test.)

"What have I done to you?" (The confident release and relinquishment to God…) Elijah was finally getting it, and resting in it. He knew where the responsibility belonged. This was God's work, God's ministry, and God's plan. It isn't about us carrying that kind of load that weighs us down to the dust and leaves us weak and wondering and so overwhelmed that checking out seems the only solution to our finding rest and peace and relief. We just were never meant to carry or bear that kind of burden. Only the shoulders of God are big enough for that!

"So Elisha left him and went back. He took his yoke of oxen and slaughtered them. He burned the plowing equipment to cook the meat and gave it to the people, and they ate." (The commitment.)

"Then he set out to follow Elijah and ministered to him." (The provision.)

Let me finish up by saying something here. Not too long afterwards God took Elijah to be with Himself, and a question arose. *"Where is the Lord God of Elijah?"*
Is He with me? Or not?
Do I really possess or can I truly enjoy the same provision? An excellent and very appropriate question!

The answer is the same for us today as it was for Elijah back then - He's here, now, with me, in me, over me, surrounding me…And for me!

Elijah left the legacy of his mantle as a token for Elisha. God left us One better - the legacy of His very Son! And then the descent and promise of His Own Holy Spirit upon us,

Helping us,
Comforting us,
Teaching us,
Revealing His Truth to us,
Lighting our darkness!

It's all there; we don't have to remain in despair for very long at all. My prayer for each of us is that in our times of doubt or grief or overwhelming circumstances - wherever we find ourselves - that we may come to the place where God brought Elijah in his distress, the place where God reveals Himself as all that He is and always was and all that He wants to be to us -
faithful, patient, gentle, merciful, kind,
all wise, all knowing, all sufficient,
and completely, entirely able and willing for whatever the need or task at hand, no matter how great!
May we always remember that no matter how deep our despair, the arm of God is certainly long enough to reach down to me, even there. The Lord God of Elijah is with us!

Helps

A closing word here on this subject: Depression, on some level, is common to the human experience, but it should not be left to itself. Learn what triggers it and take proper precautions. Take extra care of yourself physically. Proper diet, exercise, and medication, when indicated, will all help to alleviate the symptoms of depression. Allowing yourself to become overtired and exhausted in the healing process will only complicate it. While some level of depression may be unavoidable altogether, we can certainly learn what we *can* do to lessen its affects upon us.

Give yourself a break. Do what you can to reduce the stress level in your life, especially while you are in the midst of the healing process. Stress not only creates, but exacerbates, many of the physical ailments that so many survivors struggle with, such as Fibromyalgia, migraines, female organ problems such as ovarian cysts, yeast infections, urinary tract problems, abdominal and bowel problems, eating disorders, and other complications that are common for sexual abuse survivors, in particular. There is an interesting article on this subject on a website by Linda Halliday-Sumner, a sexual abuse consultant in Canada, that can be found at http://www.breakingthesilence.com/physical.html

Exercise your ability to choose. Refuse to remain in bondage. Fight victimization. Reject the whole victim mentality role. We can fight it and refuse it, once we understand it. Unfortunately, this is much easier said than done, mainly because many of us don't realize we're trapped in it. Kat describes it this way:

> You know what I find for myself? Sometimes I'm so "stuck" in this mindset that I don't have the discernment to recognize what is actually going on. I tend to be a bit thick when it comes to that because it's so ingrained. So, for me, personally, it's incredibly helpful when someone spells out exactly what victimization looks like (obviously the more subtle everyday things - I'm not talking about obvious physical abuse here) and what the victim mentality actually is with lots of practical, everyday examples on how to recognize it. What can I say? What's an appropriate way to act or

Just Before Dawn

think? I've discovered that at times when I am faced with a situation where I actually think to myself, "I should be saying 'no' or protecting myself," that I don't have a clue how to do it in an appropriate way. How on earth does one recognize it? Give me concrete examples on how I can deal with it once I do recognize it!

Let's do that, then. What do we mean by "victim mentality"? If we used psychological terms like "learned helplessness," we might come close to the idea. Learned helplessness can be defined as a "learned state" resulting from exposure to harmful, unpleasant situations in which there is no possibility of escape or avoidance. To carry that a step further, when we have learned these lessons through abuse and constant victimization, especially as children, we will *naturally* think like victims. The word victim is defined in Webster's Dictionary (1987) as, "one harmed by circumstances or conditions." We most certainly have been that! *BUT we don't have to continue to be!* The victim mentality, however, says that we do. It requires that if and when someone is hurt, or rejected, or left out, or in pain, or being hurt, or has to suffer defeat, it must be that she is the one who is "supposed" to be the victim. Such beliefs can be extremely, deeply ingrained. One abuse "victim" puts it this way:

"In every situation there is a winner and a loser, and the loser had better be me! *That's* the rule!"

God, however, counters that way of thinking. The word of God refutes such cruel lies over and over, inviting our perspective to be drawn upward instead. He always longs for His people to rise to their call to be the people of the Most High King and to walk in all the dignity that this identity as His people allows us to enjoy and walk in. *"And the Lord has declared this day that you are His people, His treasured possession...and that you will be a people holy to the Lord your God"* (Deut. 26:18-9). When we fall into old ways of thinking we tend to believe in (and then act upon) the contrary; we tend to look for the scraps instead of the feast because that has been our experience in the past. The "old messages" determine our actions and choices and only serve to "prove" what we were taught before (the

Helps

old self-fulfilling-prophecy-thing). It's a very sad, painful, and disappointing way to exist.

Here are some typical ways we show signs of victim mentality:

- It doesn't matter what I think. It's best just to go along and keep the peace. (*I will be shamed if I speak.*)

- If I say something, it will just make him/her mad. (*I will be punished if I upset someone.*)

- That's just the way it is. There's nothing I can do about it. (*I will be hurt worse if I resist.*)

- It's better if I get hurt than somebody else. (*I deserve to be in pain.*)

- I don't have any other choice. (*I will be without help or resources if I try to change things.*)

- I can't do it on my own. (*I am weak and incompetent.*)

- Nobody else would want me anyway. (*I'm as worthless as I feel.*)

- I will die if I try to get away. (*I am at the mercy of someone else's "Rules."*)

- No one would help me even if I asked. (*I will always be without love and protection.*)

So where *is* the way out? However it may appear to us, there is <u>always</u> a way. There are always choices! We must be determined, first of all, to remember to never reckon without God in the picture. *"I am the Lord,"* He reminded His people again and again. *"Is anything too hard for the Lord"* (Gen 18:14)? *"I will even make a way in the wilderness, and rivers in the desert"* (Isa. 42:16, 43:19). The first place to start is by deciding to allow God to change our

Just Before Dawn

minds about those things we have been wrongly led to believe. We must be willing to do battle with the enemy of our souls who has lied to us again and again until we became convinced. Let's give God equal time and access to our thought processes! We can become truly transformed as we switch (no pun intended) loyalties, as we turn *to God* to tell us what is true and what is not true. We must toss out the "Old Rule Book" and exchange it for the one that brings life and hope and transformation - the living Word of God. Romans 12:1-2 gives us the pattern to follow:

*"I appeal to you therefore, brethren, and beg of you in view of all the mercies of God, to make a decisive dedication of your bodies - presenting all your members and faculties **(to God)**...and do not be conformed any longer to this world...but be transformed and changed by the entire renewal of your mind - by its new ideals and its new attitude - so that you may prove for yourselves what is the good and acceptable and perfect will of God, even the thing which is good and acceptable and perfect in His sight, for you!"*
(Rom. 12:1,2 Amplified Version).

Begin very simply by trying something small and being willing to step out in new directions, one step at a time.

Employ the appropriate use of the word "No". Many of us would be quick to say that we aren't able to say no; that we cannot deny anyone else having his or her way over us. This simply isn't true. Think about how often we have said no - to ourselves! *No, I will not take care of myself! No, I will not rest, even when I'm tired. No, I will not call someone for prayer or support! No, I will not allow myself the time I need to exercise, eat properly, take a nap, get counseling, journal, spend some time alone with God, have coffee with a friend, read a good book, go to a Bible study, relax and have fun, or give myself a break. No, no, NO!* You see? We are often quite good at saying no; the problem is that we are not using our *"no"* appropriately or directing it properly. The key for any of us is balance and moderation.

Helps

When something is not good for us, we need to recognize it, with help if necessary (it usually is), and find better ways to function and do life. Because we cannot be fair or objective when it comes to matters concerning ourselves, we need others to help, to hold us up, and to keep us on the right track. Once we become aware of the possible pitfalls in the path, we can then take steps (sometimes literally) to redirect our course so that we can avoid them. *Sometimes we get so caught up and distracted by the things we cannot do that we forget or neglect to do the things we can.* We *do* have choices, *always* - they may not be easy ones or the ones we would prefer, but we have them. *We aren't little and powerless anymore! We do not have to be anybody's victim, not ever again!*

Learn about setting healthy boundaries. Poor boundaries are a huge problem for many of us, and we have some fuzzy ideas about what setting boundaries is all about. Cloud and Townsend explain, "Boundaries define us. They show what is me and what is not me. A boundary shows me where I end and someone else begins, leading me to a sense of ownership" (*Boundaries* 29). Boundaries are not something we set for or put around other people, they are for us. "Boundaries, not bulwarks, fences, not walls - there is a difference" (32). Fences around our property need gates so that we can let out the bad when it is inside and let in the good in when it is outside. We need to keep things that will nurture us inside our fences and keep the things that will harm us outside. We cannot control what other people do, but we can take care of the things within our own safe boundary lines. *Boundaries*, the book by Henry Cloud and John Townsend, is a wonderful resource for help in getting this issue straight for the boundary impaired!

Learn to play. This may sound strange to some, but for those who weren't *allowed* to play this is a bigger challenge than the average person can imagine. It is important to learn to play, however, and should be considered a part of the healing process. Playing is not only beneficial to our physical bodies, it is a good way for us to relieve stress and other pent up emotions. Laughter is healing. Fun is relieving. Joy is strengthening. *"The joy of the Lord is your strength,"* Nehemiah reminds us (8:10). When we have a reservoir of

Just Before Dawn

joy to draw from, it will serve to sustain us when those things that steal our joy threaten to overwhelm us. Playing is also a way to learn to laugh at life and to smile at ourselves once in a while (working at healing can be pretty serious business sometimes, to say the least!); this is especially essential for those of us who have had to take life too seriously as a result of our past experiences.

Breathe. Breathe in life. Find what brings you life and breath it deeply in! Take time to heal, to process, to stop and focus on the things you need to do in order to recover from the damaging effects of abuse upon your heart, your mind, your body, your soul, and your very being. I read somewhere once that breathing in deeply and holding your breath for 20 seconds is "like holding the hand of God" because of the benefits to the physical body (it was an article by a physician). Try it. Give yourself permission to take the time you need to learn to do this, to grow, to rest, and to be restored. Healing is a process, but process is something which God Himself uses for all that He has given life to. Be patient. Breathe in God's life right where you are, wherever you are, and don't miss out on the things He wants to show you as you travel on the healing path toward wholeness with Him. It is well worth it!

Don't neglect the spiritual aspect in the healing process. Discover Who the true Lord Jesus Christ, the One and only Son of the Most High God, is. Come to know God for Who He *really* is. Learn the true meaning of *father* as God intended it. For too many of us, this whole concept has been devastatingly distorted. The psalmist refers to Him again and again as his Shepherd, his Strength and Song, his Help, Rock, Shield, Protector, Keeper, Light and Salvation, Fortress, Deliverer, Guide (and more!). If we have come to believe any other thing about God, it is most often the result of our experiences with other people or things that we have confused with Him. *Set out on a quest for Truth; seek Him, and be determined to know the whole truth about Who He is, what He says, what He desires for His people, and what He does and does not do.* When we begin to see God for Who He really is, for Who *He* (rather than the deceiver of our souls) says He is, we will have left behind those people and things the enemy has used in our lives to accuse Him to us and cause the separation

Helps

between us that leaves such a void in our hearts and lives. Donna wrote this after learning about "what makes God smile" from a devotional:

> A love based relationship with God? My relationship with Him has always been fear based. I have always been afraid to trust Him, somehow thinking that if I somehow drew His attention towards me, He would hurt me, "for my own good." Pretty silly to think I could creep around being obedient enough to not draw attention to myself, to maintain some sort of status quo, without "rocking the boat" by displaying overt sin or noisy anger (or even happiness). I must look like the two-year-old who crouches down behind something that is much smaller than she is, thinking that she is "hiding" behind it and not being seen. The thought of having God's complete attention all of the time is a very uncomfortable one. How often is He really pleased with me compared to being disappointed or disgusted?

Only one thing will change such fear-based beliefs. We must come to know God intimately for ourselves, so that we cannot be fooled by accusations against Him or defamation of His character by the enemy who is so deeply invested in keeping us far from Him.

<u>Guard against Inner Lies.</u> An essential aspect that must not be neglected in order for our healing to occur is the part that spiritual warfare plays. We cannot afford to "look the other way" and live our lives as if we are not engaged in a very intense spiritual battle when it comes to breaking free from the lies that our past experiences have taught us. We need to be able to recognize the lies that the enemy hurls at us and assaults us with so that we can fight back with the Truth *according to the True and Living God.* Some of those "inner lies" that many of us struggle with, to name a few, sound something like this:

- *Because of my experiences I will always be just damaged goods.*

Just Before Dawn

- *I will never be lovable or acceptable to God or anyone else.*

- *I deserve to be hurt.*

- *Bad things only happen to bad people.*

- *I will never be healed. It will always be like this.*

- *Because I lack sufficient faith, God will not help me.*

- *God is displeased with my weaknesses and fears. He's tired of my failures.*

- *I don't belong to the human race, and what applies to others doesn't apply to me.*

- *If anyone ever found out about my past, they would know how bad I really am.*

- *If I speak out or break my silence, I will be destroyed.*

- *I am responsible for the bad things that happen to those I love.*

- *If I tell about my abuse, I will be exposed as a liar and a fraud.*

- *God doesn't want me to focus on any of this. I need to "forget" what lies behind.*

- *I need to have more faith, pray harder, try more, and get on with being a "victorious Christian."*

- *I need to stop wasting time and resources on myself when they should be applied to saving the world.*

Helps

- *Taking care of myself is selfish and greedy.*

- *I am inherently evil and bad.*

- *I will never fit in or belong.*

- *If I remember what happened to me I will die.*

- *I am beyond repair.*

<u>Break all unhealthy bonds and ties with those who would seek to keep you living by the "Old Rules."</u> The "Old Rules" are those (often unspoken) creeds that we developed as we were growing up and learning to exist in our abusive circumstances. The Old Rules were necessary for survival then; they kept us safe and they taught us what to do and not to do in an unpredictable world. The problem comes, though, in letting go of the Old Rules when they are no longer truly needed. This is an incredibly difficult thing to do, for, after all, we have trusted them to preserve us! Clinging to the Old Rules, however, will hinder our healing and stunt our growth. God wants to help us establish *New Rules!*

Be aware, though, that this may not make everybody around us entirely happy, to say the least! Change is difficult for most people, not just for abuse survivors. If we have surrounded ourselves with those who are also invested in keeping the Old Rules intact we will have even more difficulty and conflict when we try to "switch loyalties." We must be willing to risk breaking old habits and unhealthy ties to the ways we handled life in the past. That may include establishing new and healthier relationships. When we are "bonded" to something or someone in an unhealthy way, those bonds must be broken by prayerfully renouncing and forsaking them. Find safe prayer support from those who are spiritually mature and who know and love God. Charles Kraft has written some excellent books on warfare prayer and healing prayer, which might prove helpful. Neil Anderson's *Steps to Freedom in Christ* may also be a good source of doing the spiritual housekeeping that all believers coming to Christ can benefit from.

Seek help for addictive behaviors. Addictions include and involve more than substance abuse (drugs, alcohol, prescription medications, etc). Eating disorders are not something that should be taken lightly. Anorexia and bulimia are life threatening and can have long lasting consequences in more ways than one. Self-injury, such as cutting, burning, and other forms of self-inflicted pain and "punishment" can also be extremely addicting. It is entirely possible to feel addictive compulsions for abusive relationships, promiscuity, and other "acting out" types of behavior. Take these issues seriously, as they can lead to more than temporary "relief" by scarring or becoming numbed out of your mind! Don't attempt to overcome addictions alone. Seek counsel, get an accountability partner, or join a support group where someone knowledgeable and experienced can help you with these vital issues.

Resist the tendency to isolate. Establishing healthy relationships by "prayerfully selecting" (as one friend of mine puts it) safe people to be in your life is the first essential step. To try to endure the incredible losses we have sustained as a result of abuse is asking far more than we are capable of handling! Because abuse occurred within relationships, healing must happen within relationships, too. The difference now is that we can choose the kind of relationships we will and will not be in. As one survivor puts it, "We are not little any longer!" So, we *do* have the freedom and responsibility to make wise decisions about who we share our lives and the issues of our hearts with. That means we need to be wise and discerning in this whole area of relationships. We need to teach ourselves how to choose to be surrounded by safe people; we need to be with those whom we wish to be like (I Cor. 15:33). As abuse survivors, most of us have a pretty good idea of what that looks like…or do we?

Helps

Establishing Healthy Relationships

What do safe people look like? How do we avoid getting into unwholesome and "co-dependent" relationships with those who are not safe? *Safe People,* a book by Cloud and Townsend, is one good resource to glean from on this issue. The authors list several things to look for in helping ourselves to be better equipped in choosing the types of relationships we establish with other people. For those who have spent their lives surrounded by unsafe people, it is not uncommon to find ourselves attracted to certain types of people and situations simply because they are the most familiar to us. We do need to carefully consider the kinds of relationships we are involved in and, after sensibly evaluating them, make the necessary changes to ensure that they are healthy ones. This will certainly require some help at first, but God is up to the challenge of helping us make those kinds of decisions whenever we put Him in charge. We develop the right instincts as we learn what the standards and character of God really are like.

In the old suspense movie, *Gaslight*, Charles Boyer (the bad guy), determined to find and possess four precious jewels hidden in a house by its former owner (whom he has strangled), plots a scheme that almost works. Marrying the heiress, played by Ingrid Bergman (the victim), he persuades her to move back into the house and then proceeds to attempt to eliminate her by slowly driving her insane.

The term *gas lighting* comes from this movie. It refers to the planned process of convincing someone that she or he is crazy. It is also one of the major forms that psychological abuse takes; it subtly chips away at a person's ability to use sound logic and causes the person to not trust their own judgment anymore (Miller 1995).

The reason I mention this story is because it paints a picture for us of what an unhealthy relationship looks like *to the person who is in the midst of it*. As viewers, we knew what was going on behind the scenes (Boyer was obviously the bad guy), but for the person being "gas lighted" it may not appear to be a clear issue at all.

It is important, even essential, that we recognize the signs of an unhealthy relationship so that the cycle of abuse that typically occurs within them can be broken and/or avoided altogether. The damage that unhealthy relationships do is something we must face and make sure we are aware of so that we can act on what we know.

First, we must recognize <u>the problem</u>; we need to pay attention to the warning signs that indicate to us that we may be in an unhealthy relationship. *<u>The solution</u>* we often hear, which sounds simple enough, "get out, leave!" is not so easily done as said (for lots and lots of reasons). And finally, *the effects* of remaining in an unhealthy relationship when we do so against our better judgment can be potentially devastating.

This scenario is a common one, where a relationship begins on one level but slides slowly but surely down onto another. It doesn't even have to be in a relationship with a significant other that these dynamics can come into play. Friendships can get out of balance, as well, and cause a level of distress and turmoil that should not be occurring in a healthy one. In the next few pages, we'll briefly look at how unhealthy relationships begin and what unhealthy versus healthy relationships looks like so that we will know how to deal with this situation if we find ourselves in one.

The problem:

First, what we need to be aware of is that unhealthy (and, unfortunately, the resulting abusive) relationships very seldom start out that way. In Patricia Evans' book, *Verbal Abuse Survivors Speak Out*, she makes a point of saying that no one *plans* to get into unhealthy relationships (147-9). She tells story after story, however, of how easily this can happen. Often, it's a matter of not heeding the warning signs that flash in and out of our minds when we begin to suspect that something just isn't quite right. *"Why didn't I see it? Why didn't I listen to myself?"* is the common lament. *"I thought something was wrong with me..."* or, *"He said I was making a big deal out of nothing, that I was just being oversensitive,"* or, *"She said I just wasn't strong enough or smart enough, or didn't make enough money. Nothing I did pleased her."*

Helps

Hopefully, in sharing here just what some of those warning signs are, we can avoid getting ourselves into these kinds of unhealthy relationships and not have to go through the painful process of trying to get out of them once they have been established.

The following are some of the typical characteristics of unhealthy and potentially abusive relationships, which can include the any or all of these signs:

- An extreme need to control. This is a big warning sign. What at first is interpreted as one partner "taking care" of the other, we begin to realize is an extreme need on his or her part to control the other. An example of this might be when one demands of the other an account of her / his time, money, or relationships.

- Another warning sign is when your partner uses *manipulation through guilt to get his or her way.* You are made to feel that, if anything goes wrong in the relationship, you are at fault. There's little room for discussion in this situation.

- Losing all sense of who you are as an individual apart from who you are as a couple or friend. When you find that you must conform to the other's idea of what you "should" like or dislike, how you "should" be, act, dress, feel, or think, etc.

- When the partner becomes angry or jealous and discourages the other from spending time with friends or family, or doing activities that don't include him or her.

- When the partner is overly possessive, as if you no longer have any life or rights apart from the other.

- When you became afraid of making him or her angry and fear disapproval in even the littlest things.

- When you feel like you can't make any plans, decisions, or even simple choices without checking with the other first.

- When you get the cold shoulder or the silent treatment if you don't always agree.

<u>The Solution</u> involves, first of all, knowing what a balanced, healthy relationship looks like and making that our standard, our expectation, and then working to incorporate these qualities into our relationships, both existing and future.

A healthy relationship should include the following:

- First, we must realize that we cannot get our sense of worth from other people, no matter what kind of relationship we are in or how wonderful the person we are with is. No other person can meet all our needs.

- Next, we must keep healthy boundaries, knowing what belongs to whom in the relationship, and just how far we are willing to go in order to accommodate the other person's needs while taking care of ourselves in the process.

- We need to know that we each have a right to our own feelings, and are responsible for our own actions and choices, judgments, beliefs, and attitudes. It is not our responsibility to "fix" or take on what is not really ours (and what we cannot control, anyway).

- Each of us is as valuable as the other and deserves to be treated with mutual admiration, kindness and respect.

Helps

- The main thing to remember is that we <u>are</u> each free to have opinions and to make our own choices! It often comes down to refusing to be forced or manipulated into doing things just because we think or fear someone else is demanding it of us.

- Finally, learning to work on good communication is the biggest key of all. Communication requires at least two people who are engaged in the listening process.

- Listening *to each other* is essential, and developing the ability to objectively step back and hear what the other person is saying without judgment and self-justification is what transforms an unhealthy relationship into a healthy, mutually satisfying, and growing one.

Lexy had this to say at this point:

> One of the single most important things I've learned about finding a healthy relationship is realizing that I am just fine on my own. Once I realized that, I was able to find a good relationship and stop existing in an unhealthy one because of my great fear of being alone & incomplete.

What are <u>the effects</u> of applying these principles (or not)?
According to the American Psychological Association, domestic violence is a very real problem in our society, and not to be taken lightly. ***Be aware that the current definition of abuse from both the legal and psychological perspectives includes the emotional components as well as the physical, because of the harm it does to its victims.*** There are so many factors that contribute to someone staying in an unhealthy relationship, but having a clear understanding and expectation of what a healthy one really looks like is half of the battle.

We need to be watchful and alert, then, in this whole area of relationships, both with one another and with our God. When we find ourselves becoming more caught up in what's happening outside of us

Just Before Dawn

in our relationships with people (and how they affect us) than what is happening inside of us in our relationship with God (and how that affects us) we're probably off course in our walk with Him. While we certainly do need to pay attention to the fruit our relationships produce in our lives, we must not allow them to rob us of what is most important: our relationship with the Living God.

Taking care of ourselves

The plane finally began heading toward the runway for takeoff. The speakers came to life and the stewardess gave last minute instructions to the disinterested passengers. She was saying something about airbags dropping down from above us, "should the cabin depressurize," at any time during the flight. "In the event this should occur and you are traveling with a child or someone dependent upon you or needing assistance," she instructed us, "place the mask firmly *over your own mouth first*, and *then* assist the person traveling with you." The accompanying film vignette showed happy, calm, smiling people doing this. I remember the first time I heard this, thinking indignantly, *I would never do such a selfish thing! Why, put an air mask on myself and leave my poor, helpless child struggling for breath? What kind of mother do these people think I am?!*

Well, let's think about that. Have you ever heard what oxygen deprivation is like? The symptoms include confusion, light-headedness, numbness, and loss of consciousness. So, practically speaking, if in my nervous, adrenaline-hyped fumbling to get an oxygen mask on a panicking, screaming child, I keel over from lack of oxygen myself, what help have I really been? Sometimes the very best thing I can do for those around me is to take care of myself just as responsibly as I can *and then* attempt to help them.

I read somewhere once that scientists have yet to discover how to invent a machine capable of perpetual motion - there is no such thing as a car or machine or any other thing that does not eventually run out of fuel or require some type of regular maintenance. Yet, we send our cars in to be serviced more regularly than we do our own bodies.

Helps

The purpose of this section isn't to provide another list of things to do in order to fix yourself more quickly so you can get back to fixing everyone else! It's about rest, renewal, and acceptance of our humanity and our physical, emotional, and spiritual limitations. It's about acceptance of ourselves as God created us, and acceptance of His provisions for us according to His mind and His way of doing things.

We must do our part, then, to get enough rest, to eat a balanced diet, to exercise. We need to be under the care of safe, understanding physicians that can help us with the physical aspects of the healing process.

Insomnia, for example, is a common problem for those who struggle with fear at nighttime. Hyper-vigilance, exaggerated startle response, fear of someone taking advantage of us while we are asleep, internal noise and switching for those with dissociative disorders, are all common problems that contribute to our inability to sleep. Sleep deprivation can exacerbate the flashbacks, nightmares, and startle responses many of us already struggle with. Consult with your physician if sleep is a problem; there are medications that can often help and bring relief. Getting sufficient rest is absolutely essential.

Another problem common to many of us is eating disorders. Anorexia and bulimia can be serious health threats if ignored or left untreated. What is important here is to get to the root of what is causing the disorder, not just treating the symptoms. Is anorexia or bulimia simply a fear of getting fat? No way! Most often, food issues are far more complex, and painfully connected with past abuse.

Exercise is beneficial, not only in reducing stress and allowing a safe outlet for pent up energy, but has been shown to be an effective source of relief in dealing with depression because it literally alters our mood.

The point is to do what we can do to help ourselves through the difficult stages of the healing process.

Just Before Dawn

Learning to Accept Help

Allow God to work by accepting the support of those He uses in our lives to bring health and healing. We are *ALL* only a part of the Body of Christ. We were never meant to function alone and without the help and support of others. Where did we ever get the idea that accepting help was wrong or selfish, or that it indicated some flaw of weakness that is unique to us alone? This is an incredibly distorted belief that keeps so many of us lonely and isolated when we were created for fellowship and relationship with others. God Himself wants relationship with us. We are created in His image, and we will never be satisfied with living life cut off from others and on our own.

Fight denial. To deny our needs is to reject God's design for us and to refuse His provision. We deny not only ourselves but the rest of the Body of Christ the privilege of watching God meet us in the very places that will best bring Him glory and intimacy with His people. Imagine missing out on the opportunity to exclaim joyfully, like the psalmist in Ps. 118:23, "This work is of the Lord and is His doing, and it is marvelous in our eyes!" If we have come to believe (or experience) that admitting to having needs will bring us rejection from our families, communities, or churches, then we are missing the mark when it comes to the whole purpose of being a part of the body of Christ. Instead of living in healthy interdependence with one another, we will be relating to one another in the bondage of fear, rather than the freedom Christ died to give us.

Know and accept your limitations. Remember, we are each *only a part* of the Body of Christ. We are *not supposed* to be able to do it on our own! So, what part are you? What is it that God has uniquely called you to be? I shared the following at a seminar I spoke at once:

Helps

My Part in the Body of Christ

I'm a liver. I tend to filter everything. I like my hiding place back here behind the ribs.
I'm a scribe. I love words, to write, taking things in account and see where they fit and balance out. I love order and organizing thoughts and ideas and the things I hear and ponder.
I'm a servant. I want to be like Jesus.
I'm an intercessor, a worshipper, a counselor, a teacher…

I don't know what part I am!

But one thing I do know -
We cannot know our part or function (which go together, because a part in itself is of no use unless it functions and does what it was created to do) in the body of Christ until we know who we are because of the finished work of Jesus Christ on our behalf. Sometimes, that's the greatest service we can do for both ourselves and the rest of the body.

Before I go any further, there are a couple of definitions I want to give you.
These are two words I want to concentrate on, because I'll be using them as I share more with you:

Fragmentation: *Disintegration, collapse. Pieces (of a whole). Break down of function.*

Function: *Special purpose or task of a machine, person, or bodily part.*
In working order. Operational.
The action or activity proper to a person.
A factor related to or dependent upon other factors
(one of the elements contributing to a particular result).

Just Before Dawn

For me the journey of coming to know my part in the Body of Christ began in earnest with a question - II Tim 4:5: *"What is my ministry?"*

I asked that question for years before the answer finally began to really dawn on me, but it came in a way I never expected. The vehicle for getting me there was a mode of transportation I never wanted to travel on. Before I knew it, the journey was under way, ready or not; the outcome, however, was well worth it.

I suppose it began with a desire, a longing. I wanted, though I would have never had the courage to say it out loud, to minister to God's people in a way that would really make a difference for good. I wanted to serve God, but thought that was only reserved for an elite and treasured few, so I began to ask God to at least make me a woman of prayer so I could somehow be a source of blessing to those who were serving God, "in the way I probably wouldn't qualify," for. He did, but as God, in His own way, takes the longings and desires of our hearts (that He put there anyway) and puts us in places we never expected, we find that He does the very thing we were so afraid to ask.

That was the year God put me into the ministry with Freedom in Christ. After a period of training, I began to lead people through the Steps, but what I discovered in that process was not so much about the Steps themselves or even the good, solid principles they communicated; I began to learn so much about myself as I came alongside people who were hurting. This was especially true when it came to abuse survivors, for though I had no conscious memory at that time of my own abuse issues, *I realized that I knew* what those people were talking about, and I could definitely relate to and minister to their pain in some wonderful and supernatural way. It was awesome, and for the first time in twenty plus years of asking and wondering if I could ever be of any good use to God or

His people I felt like I finally knew my calling; I finally knew what my ministry was!

That was the beginning of a long, difficult process for me, because it helped me to understand just how out of touch and clueless I was about the depth of my own pain and woundedness, at least (or perhaps especially) from a spiritual perspective. *All I knew was that the life I had lived and presented outside* (without really even thinking about it or realizing it) *and what I felt inside didn't match up.* IF I ever stopped long enough to actually think that through and (God forbid) *feel* the incredible loneliness and desolation that was in there, it sent me into incredible despair and intolerable feelings of inadequacy and shame, but with absolutely no understanding of why.

So, I did what a whole lot of us do to "fix" ourselves inside: I moved faster and pushed harder. I was convinced that the way to deal with that vague *but perpetual* ache inside was to "do" more, pray more, confess more, repent more, and work more, because I was sure that the problem was me. It was all my fault, due to my lack of faith or spiritual discipline or prayer; I was sure that there was absolutely no way I could possibly be doing enough. What other possible reason could there be for such wretchedness?!

And so I, too, fell into that other big trap: The Comparison Trap, always a no-win situation. "Of course" (I privately reasoned) that's why I felt so awful about myself. "Of course" that's why I felt so empty and insecure and never ever able to measure up. "Of course" that was the real problem!

The deep sense of inadequacy and unworthiness I felt convinced me I would never have any right to play any "real" part in the Body, and it drove me to despair again and again, but I was powerless to "get over it and get on." I chastened myself again and again, *"just reckon it dead, sister..."* Well, needless to say, that didn't work!

Because these kinds of beliefs and feelings of inadequacy always lead to isolation (either internally or externally), I had no other means of measuring the truth or accuracy of my perspectives or self-judgment and doubt.

The result? Deeper isolation, greater fragmentation. Pretty soon the "breakdown of function" became so obvious (at first only to me) *that I had to* deal with it, or die in the process. Desperation led me to actually stopping long enough to look inside and seeing that there was something terribly wrong. So I broke down and did the unthinkable...*I asked for help!!* (gasp!!!) I used resources available through other parts in the Body, and as a result I found a whole world of resources suddenly coming to life inside of me. So began my journey into healing and restoration to wholeness.

What I had to come to terms with first was how really fragmented and cut off I was; not just from the rest of the Body of Christ, but from myself, *and even* (though outwardly I was doing "all the right stuff") *from my God*.

Luke 11:17 says that every kingdom divided against itself is brought to desolation and cannot stand. That was me. I cannot begin to express adequately what that feels like.

From then on it was a do-or-die proposition: no turning back. I absolutely, positively HAD to know the truth about the things I believed and the things that really were *from God's perspective* (not people's).

So what's a square peg in a world of round holes to do?
Turn to the Maker of them both! And so my quest began. As I made my desperate search for God and Truth, this is (some of) what I found out:

Helps

The most important part about being a part of the body of Christ is not the part itself, but the Power behind the functioning of that part!

That means we've got to know what the word of God teaches on the subject and to come to know the divine intention and character of the God Who created the Body.

<u>Question:</u> How many times do we find ourselves, when presented with questions about what our part or our function or ministry or contribution in and/or to the Body of Christ, do we catch ourselves thinking one thing but perhaps saying something else?

For example, most of us wouldn't have any problem answering this question with a bold (but humble, of course!) comment like, "Well, I'm really good at the gift of serving, or helping, or hospitality, or setting up chairs, or scrubbing toilet bowls." I mean, after all, it would be really proud and presumptuous to say anything else (Wouldn't it?!).

What we do when we deny our hearts an expression and an outlet is to keep them in bondage, which is the very thing that Christ died to rescue us from. David said when he kept silence he wasted away with groanings. God gave His people voice. When we lose our voice, we lose our identity, our individuality, and the opportunity of being known; we miss out on fellowship, on the uniting bonds that help us form those cohesive relationships. We miss out on those strengths and gifts that the other parts of the Body have to contribute to our lives for our good and for theirs!

So, how do we get there? How do we get past those distressing issues that keep us bound up and hinder us from entering into all that God wants us to experience as we *<u>inter-depend</u>* on one another?

There are so many passages like the one in Jeremiah 1 that we could point out to you but let's use this as an example. Note the emphasis here -

"Before *I* formed you
I knew you
I sanctified you
I ordained you
Whatsoever *I* command you that shall you speak
Be not afraid…for *I am* with you
I will deliver you
I have put *My* words in thy mouth
I have this day *set thee* over…to…
I will hasten *My* word to perform it
I will call all the families of the kingdoms
I will utter *My* judgments
Thou therefore gird up thy loins, and arise, and speak unto them all that I command thee
For, behold (look!), *I have made thee* this day a defended city…
I am with thee to deliver thee!

It's all about God and His power, strength and abilities, not ours!
<u>That's the point!</u> This is **His** work, **His** ministry, **and His** people.

If our hearts are in it and we're available to come on His terms we qualify. That's it! (What a relief!!)

<u>So what is my part in the Body of Christ?</u>

I remember hearing a news story not too long ago about a young boy whose arm had been bitten off by a shark. A family member immediately jumped in the water and beat on the shark until it released the severed limb, and then sent it to the hospital with the boy where doctors reattached it.

Helps

Amazing! The fact that anyone should consider that one part of the boy's body so important that he was willing to risk his own life in order to recover it is astounding! Then I wondered, when I see a part of the Body of Christ separated from the rest, what am I willing to do in order to see it restored? Am I that brave, dedicated, committed, willing-hearted, and courageous? Do I see the value and worth of *every* part of the Body of Christ the way God does?

When a member of the body is severed and separated from the rest of the body, it dies. Period. So what's my attitude about that? When I see me, or someone outside of me, apart from the whole, what is my response? Just how willing am I to go the extra mile to see to it that that member is restored? Am I convinced that every part, every member is essential, *absolutely, positively, functionally essential* to whatever it is God wants to accomplish through my union with that member?

We must be willing to search our hearts, search our minds, attitudes, opinions and prejudices, and then search the scriptures and make sure that our hearts and minds are in unity with His plan and purpose and intention.

Ephesians 4

I therefore beseech you (appeal to and beg you) to walk (lead a life) worthy of the divine calling to which you have been called - with behavior that is a credit to the summons to God's service...

Be eager and strive earnestly to guard and keep the harmony and oneness produced by the Spirit in the binding power of peace.

There is one body and one Spirit, just as there is also one hope that belongs to the calling you (all) received,...and One God and Father of us all, Who is above all, sovereignly over all, pervading all and living in us all.

Yet grace, God's unmerited favor, was given to each of us individually - not indiscriminately, but in different ways - in proportion to the measure of Christ's rich and bounteous gift.

And His gifts were varied; He Himself appointed and gave men to us, some to be apostles (special messengers), some prophets, some pastors (shepherds of His flock) and teachers.

His intention was the perfecting and the full equipping of His saints (consecrated people), that they should do the work of ministering toward building up Christ's body,

That it might develop until we all attain oneness in the faith and in the comprehension of the full and accurate knowledge of the Son of God.

Trying to really pin down my particular gift or "part in the Body" is still difficult for me; I suppose this is because, for so many years I felt it was my job to do it all and not rely on anybody else to do it for me. There are so many wonderful choices to pick from! What a huge load of responsibility I felt! What bondage!

I've come to this determination:

We are *all* in process; none of us have arrived.
And God is in the process, too, of bringing many sons to righteousness,
of conforming us to the image of His Son.

But without *you*, eyes, I won't be able to see that clearly enough to know the way.
And without *you*, ears, I may not hear clearly - I may miss out on something wonderful that He has to say.

Without *you*, feet, how can I get there?
Without *you*, arms, who will support me?

I'm inviting each of you, then.
Join me. Come alongside me. Don't leave me alone and to my own devices. Uphold me, encourage me, point me to Christ! And as I learn and glean from you, I will have some gift to return to you or pass on what you have done and been for me to someone else that I wouldn't have had to give to them otherwise.

The result?
I'll be so much more than a limb, a fragment, a puzzle piece. My walking and functioning in wholeness will paint you a picture to marvel at and enjoy, and through the whole wonderful miraculous process of functioning as I was created to do, you will be blessed, and our God will be glorified.

A word to therapists, counselors, lay support people, and family members:

A final word in this section is to those who wish (or have been drafted!) to come alongside abuse survivors in their healing process. Often, we come with the best intentions when we think of how the hurting ones among us need our encouragement and support, but that may not be enough. We need to know, first and foremost, that we are in this work because God has called us and gifted us to do it. We need to be loving and responsible enough to be sure that we are appointed and equipped by God to the extent that we are able to be. Healing from trauma, especially when the nature of that trauma is spiritual and sexual abuse, is difficult work and requires time and commitment for both helpers and survivors. God will have to be the One to supply the grace for all of us to see the healing process through.

As we come alongside those seeking help and healing, we will have to come to terms with our own issues so that we do not unintentionally do harm to either ourselves or those we are hoping to minister to. Pray about your particular level of involvement in this process, in whatever capacity God would have you enter into. Do not assume that your experience or degree automatically qualifies you for this particular type of work. Know your own limitations, what you can and cannot handle, and share the work with others who will come alongside you, as well. And then be fiercely honest with how and why you do come alongside others to help. For example, if you are *never* available outside of office hours, why? And if you are *always* available, why? These are heart-searching questions. God is interested in bringing health and wholeness to *all* of the parts of the body of Christ, and so we must jealously guard that essential connection to Him if we are to be conduits of healing for God's people. Some things simply cannot be learned from a book; they must (more importantly) be lived out. Linda wrote the following about her counselor:

> *In her eyes, we find*
> *Kindness, that permits us to speak,*
> *Commitment, that lets us take risks,*
> *Caring, that soothes our fears,*
> *Honesty, which allows us to stop playing games;*
> *Understanding, allowing us to go on;*
> *And*
> *Love...that doesn't go away.*
>
> *In her arms, we find*
> *Strength, providing us with a chance to let go or to fight;*
> *Tenderness, that we have never known;*
> *Comfort, to help us be still,*
> *Safety, to finally just be,*
> *Protection, holding us together;*
> *And*
> *Love...which continues to heal.*
>
> *In her words, we find*
> *Reassurance, in the repetition of familiar expressions;*

Stability, with the truth always being told;
Peace, in just hearing her voice;
Gentle challenges, to keep us growing;
Affirmation, guiding us through every step
And
Love…that changes our lives forever.

I notice that Linda wrote nothing about her therapist's education, knowledge, or special abilities as a professional! What she wrote about is this dear counselor's heart. I have summarized below a small portion of what Dr. Diane Langberg had to say in her excellent address to both lay and professional counselors at a recent AACC conference:

> God's call to the church is that He challenges us to face the lies that the traumatized have been taught with the truths of redemption. We cannot found our help to them on the denial that cruelty happens, nor must we attempt to minimize its effects. Any redemption that fails to take evil into account is no redemption. Jesus Christ himself, Who entered into the terrible evil of this fallen world, has invited us to enter into the rubble of shattered lives with Him…This work requires that we know how to do this (helping) work well. *If you go into the lives of those who have been traumatized ignorant of the impact of abuse you will harm those already damaged by it*…This means we need to understand trauma and how it affects human lives. It means we need to know how to respond to frightened human beings who have been overwhelmed by atrocity. And it means persevering, because the effects of trauma in people's lives far outlast the events that caused it.

Healing takes time. These things all take time: developing good social skills, living with appropriate boundaries, functioning on a day-to-day basis (in a way, for example, that those who grew up with healthy role models and who experienced nurturing and love and security already do without thinking too much about it). Learning to trust, to grow in healthy relationships with others, to have friends and to be a friend, is a process. Who will show them how? Friesen (et al) writes this in *Living From the Heart Jesus Gave You*:

> People need to know who they are. They also need to be reminded who they are, frequently, by those who love them, and really know them. And they need repair, so that they can live from the hearts Jesus gave them. That is what it takes to achieve wholeness in a fractured world. It takes belonging to a community. It takes a whole lot of work in the area of maturity. It takes God's hand to boost people when they are stuck, and it takes a lifetime."

The call of God to the church is to, *"strengthen the feeble minded, support the feeble hearted,"* and yet, we find ourselves ill equipped and afraid. God Himself calls us to the work of helping and building up one another. What hinders us?

Finding the answer requires a searching of *our own* hearts first. Do we struggle with superiority and pride? Are we under the impression that those who are struggling in their ability to cope with what has happened in their lives are somehow lacking in fortitude or faith in some way that "the rest of us" are not? Or, perhaps, do we fear those unhealed areas of our own lives, which are being touched?

When we come alongside and help others, we will find out things about ourselves that we never knew before. We will find our own issues exposed, our selfishness and pride and superiority and complacency and impatience and lack of love will soon come to the surface. We will feel overwhelmed at the need around us if we look, and will have to admit our powerlessness to fix it. We will become blaringly aware of our own weaknesses and limitations. We will become vulnerable to the despair and darkness that trauma and suffering and abuse have brought into the lives of those we are ministering to. And it will touch us, just as it touches the heart of God.

Helps

But, if we allow it to happen, the suffering of others will also drive *us* to the Healer because we will become convinced once and for all that we are not the healers; we are not the wise counselors; we are not the towers of strength that we prefer to think we are. We will come to a knowledge of the Most High God in a way we never could have otherwise.

Helping Hurting People

"Alas for those that never sing but die with all their music in them."
Oliver Wendell Holmes

Every person you meet has a song within them; one they were meant by their Creator to sing!

When you look at that wounded, hurting person sitting across from you, *what do you see?* What do you believe *God* for - concerning them?

Even before we step into the counseling room or the place of helping and support we need to know the answer to this question. How? *By seeing every person we come into contact with through the eyes of Christ, aware that they were created in the image of God Himself and their lives were ordained by Him.*

Let me tell you a very short, short story:

> *Once upon a time, I don't know when, but one day, there was a declaration in heaven, an announcement of sorts. It was a determination made by the King of kings Himself, the Creator and the Father of all eternity, that a new life was to be spoken into being. And with His word, it was done. This is where it (this life) began.*
>
> *The fact that, for a time at least, this particular life would be in the hands of cruel and evil men could not alter eternity's plan for that life, nor could it undo and cancel out the*

sovereign good will and kind intent of God for that life. In the end, no matter what befell that life that had been spoken into being, Love Himself would prevail.

Do you see the point? God willed for each life to be lived wholly and abundantly. Free will means that some of those lives that God has good intentions for will be hurt by those driven by the one whose only intention is to kill and destroy all that God means for good. What is our response, then, to be?

Sometimes, we humans miss it. We forget or are ignorant of our true heritage. We forget our true identity.

We also forget that we have been called and commissioned to be a part of God's solution and provision for restoration. What we often forget, most sadly, is that WE are not the solution. God is.

If we turn to Acts 3, we will see a model of what an effective people-helper looks like:

The Roles Acts 3:1-10

The servant could only give to others what he had himself received and taken hold of (about Who Christ was and what that meant both to him and to others) *experientially.*

The Issue Acts 3:11-12

We do not have the talents, the resources, or the ability in ourselves to make any body spiritually or even physically whole. *We aren't that powerful; we aren't that holy!*
But God is.

Yes, we can share with them what God has given to us. We can reach out our hand and offer to support and help lift them up, but only God can make an ankle bone strong. Never, never forget that! It is not

Helps

about you and me; *it is all about Who He is to you and me* - because of Who He is Himself!

The Answer Acts 3:16

The Name of Jesus Christ, of Jehovah Nissi, God my Healer, and faith in all that His Name is - this is what brings about wholeness and healing (Ps. 103:1-6). When you and I get this issue really settled within our deepest, innermost selves, we can point others to Him in the confidence that comes with knowing that *we know* Who God really is and what He's about when it comes to the Great Physician's business of restoring and making whole and healing hurting hearts.

"For God is not unrighteous to forget your work and labor of love that you have shown toward His name, in that you have ministered to the saints, and do minister" (Heb. 6:10).

A final word, and perhaps the highest focus of all:

> *"And God will wipe away all tears from their eyes.*
> *And there will be no more death, nor mourning, nor*
> *crying out, nor will there be any more pain;*
> *for the first things are passed away" (Rev. 21:4).*

Just Before Dawn

The Battle

*"For every provocation against God's
cause there is a provision for victory."*
R. Arthur Matthews

It's a secret battle I'm engaged in, not fought on any physical battlefield. In fact, most people have no idea I'm involved in such a conflict at all. I wake in the morning and the battle is in full force. I ready myself to go out into my day, carefully putting on my "Okay Face" before I do so. I show up at work (or church, or the grocery store, or the PTA meeting, wherever) with a plastic smile, delve into the task before me with that determination that no one must know, no one must ever suspect. These things must never be spoken about - who would believe me anyway? And even if they did, who would understand? My shame and fear keep me silent, constantly engaged in the battle - alone.

How may of us live this way? How many are overwhelmed at even the thought of getting up in the morning and facing one more day of such internal turmoil and conflict - not to mention all the outside commitments and responsibilities that keep us running on fumes (who has time to stop for gas?). For those in such a quandary, it takes an incredibly intense effort to face people, work, and the endless list of daily to-dos (that cannot possibly get done in time for us to tackle the things that will surely come up that are not even on the list!) without falling prey to the internal panic raging within.

The battle began back in Genesis, when Satan came to accuse God in order to separate us from Him. The battle continues as he points God as the cause of our pain, grief, suffering, sorrows. Remember when Job's servants came running to him with the awful report of what had befallen his children? *"A fire from God came..."* Yet the fire, according to verse 19 in chapter two, was clearly caused by Satan, not God, with the clear intention of destroying Job's family and possessions. How quickly those same accusing whispers against God come when something happens that we cannot explain! God can do anything, after all - can't He? My answer to that is an emphatic *NO!*

The Battle

For example, God cannot lie (Titus 1:2). God cannot break His promises (Ps. 89:6). He cannot be tempted with evil nor tempt us (Jms. 1:13). He cannot be unfaithful (II Tim. 2:13). He cannot be any other than Who He is; He cannot stop being God (Mal. 3:6, Ps. 90:2). Because of all that and more He cannot cease to be true to His character, which is only good, only just, only pure, and only true, whether to our very limited perception and finite understanding it appears to be so or not. The Word of God reminds us that we live in a world that lays, at least for now, under the control of the evil one (I Jn. 5:19). *Let's make sure we put the credit for evil and destruction in our world right where it belongs - on the wicked one, the deceiver, the adversary of our souls, the father of all lies, the destroyer himself.*

The real battle, of course, is for the mind - our belief system - that thinking that determines the script we will follow and live by. *What we believe determines how we live.* How, then, do we not become casualties of the battle taking place around and within us, of the things we have learned and come to believe - about ourselves, our worth, our gifts, our abilities, and especially our freedom to choose?

The most difficult thing for many of us is getting past the belief that we have no choice but to remain in the unbearable places we find ourselves, that we are "stuck" with living out the consequences of the sinful choices of others against us. Think about it - how did we get here in the first place? Whatever led us to believe that we had to do it all and do it perfectly? Where does that thinking originate? To many it seems to make no sense. If you're an abuse survivor, however, it makes perfect sense. After all, who tells a child while they are being abused that their feelings matter, that their dignity matters, that their well being is valued above all else, or that if they don't like something or if something is hurting them, they should simply give the word and it will stop? Most certainly the abuser did not say any such thing! It wasn't safe to say no, it wasn't safe to say what you did and did not want or like, and it did not matter what you felt or needed or said or thought! Those messages came across crystal clear!! And so does the whole idea of not having a free choice – even now. A victim has no choice, no rights, and no freedom. Abuse occurred, and most often, the abuser was very thorough in making sure the victim felt responsible, was taught that it was his or her own fault, that it was deserved, and that somehow it was brought on by the one being abused. Whether that message was spoken or unspoken, it is one that must be quickly learned in order to survive. *In the abuse of a child, no matter what form it takes, there is never a choice for the victim.*

BUT, we are not children anymore! And now, at last, we most certainly **_can_** choose how we will and will not live, who we will and will not live with, what we will and will not allow to happen to us, what we do believe and do not believe, what we need and feel and want and like and think, o*r not*. It's our turn to pick! We can choose, finally.

What about the enemy? The enemy can interfere, distract, pressure, condemn, threaten, lie, deceive…*but he cannot stop us from choosing to turn to God* for the strength to make the right and healthy choices that are part of His good will and intention for us. Those good intentions have always been there, from the very beginning of God's calling us into being. Abuse does not disqualify us, nor does it make null and void the glorious plan and intention of God for us. That is the truth, and all the messages and lies and accusations that seek to defeat us and convince us otherwise cannot change that truth.

How is it, then, that we constantly find ourselves engaged in a continual fight? Why does the struggle continue? There are a couple of things we might consider here, but first, let's think about the methods the enemy uses to keep us entangled in the very things that God has declared us free from. To do so, we must consider the enemy's tactics, just like any good soldier engaged in a war must do.

So who is our enemy?

Who is he and what is he after? Satan is the father of all lies. In scripture he is called by many names, each one quite descriptive: the evil one, that wicked one, the accuser, the devil, deceiver, tempter, dragon, serpent, destroyer, murderer, liar, thief…

The Battle

What tactics will he likely employ in order to defeat us? His names are obvious cues! Verses like Eph. 6:12 are essential for us to understand and take hold of so that we can come to an appreciation of what we're talking about here. *"For we wrestle not against flesh and blood, but against powers and principalities and spiritual forces of darkness in high places."* While Paul reminds us in II Cor. 10 that *"the weapons of our warfare are not carnal, but spiritual..."* We need to remember that God has equipped us with all that we need so that we do not live life constantly defeated by the enemy's tactics. God has, indeed, given us everything that we need for life and godliness (II Pet. 1:3), including key information on how our enemy operates. The most liberating thing we can do for ourselves, then, and for those we love, is to come to a clear understanding and confident knowledge of *the Truth as it stands before the throne of the Most High God.* We should not only be willing, but bold about testing to see what is and is not based upon Truth concerning the things we have been taught. Satan, who would keep us from enjoying and utilizing God's provision for us, will work and attempt to defeat us. We must never forget that he is a master of deception, and that he uses all his energy to come against us and convince us of what is not true. That is his only real power. I Jn. 5:19 tells us that the whole world lies under the power of the evil one. How, then, can we defeat such a wily foe? We must find out as much as we need to know in order to not fall for his deceptive tactics.

His person. Satan was originally one of God's most privileged angels (called cherubim) and was created with great power and intelligence. Because he had free will, however, he chose to rebel against God and even sought to take His place (Isa. 14:12-14), and not much has changed to this day! As much as he would like us to believe, however, he does not possess the infinite attributes that only the Most High God possesses. He is not all-powerful, he does not know everything, and he cannot be everywhere at once; he needs his demon helpers to aid his evil intentions towards man.

His purpose. Since he did not fulfill his original purpose of glorifying service to his God and Creator, he changed all that by instead seeking to destroy and defile all that God meant for good, including His eternal plan and loving intention toward us, His people. The enemy's determined purpose now is to deceive, rob, and displace man from his privileged place and from enjoying lasting fellowship with God in any way he can. He is the ultimate counterfeit, and will not hesitate to take advantage of our lack of knowledge or understanding of the truth of Who God is or His high and holy intention for us by whatever means possible. He has no qualms whatsoever about not playing fair, and never hesitates to kick those who are down. He is in every way all that the Lord Jesus Christ is not.

His final end. The good news is that Satan's time and temporary office as the god of this world is limited. Neither he nor his destructive demon forces will be allowed to continue their foul activities forever. Until then, whether it appears to be so or not, the lion is on a leash held by the hand of God and cannot determine himself how far he can and cannot go. God alone holds that kind of power over life and death (not that liar!), and God alone will have the last word (Rev. 20:10).

Our part. Until then, it is our part to resist the evil one by submitting to God (Jms. 4:7), and actively engaging in the battle before us (II Tim. 2:3,4), refusing to any longer allow fear (Matt. 10:28) or lack of knowledge (II Cor. 2:11) to be the determining factor in it. *We are only able to <u>walk</u> in the Truth if we know it!* We therefore commit ourselves to the task before us by diligently studying the scriptures (II Tim. 2:15) and applying its truths to our lives (Jms. 1:22).

<u>Prepared for Battle</u>

It is *essential* that we realize (and accept) the fact that we *are* in a battle. Because of the enemy's hostility toward us, we must take seriously the soldier image Paul describes in II Timothy 2. As R. Arthur Matthews tells us in *Born for Battle*, "we are no longer free to play the role of civilians, living as if there were no war" (96). Let's look, then, at what scripture points to regarding the soldier's role in the battle.

The Battle

The soldier must first and foremost be willing to hear from the Captain so that he can get the direction and training he needs to fight well.

The soldier must also be strong, persevering, single-minded and committed, diligent, well informed, alert, faithful, persistent, willing to stand against opposition...*and extremely confident that he cannot do any of this alone!* "And **the Lord** shall deliver me from every evil work, and will preserve me unto His heavenly kingdom..." (II Tim 4:18). What a relief! Once again we come to realize that it is not about us, it's all about Jesus, the Captain of our salvation.

> *In the inevitable clash with the powers of evil arrayed to overthrow the work of God, no assumed authority will avail. Going through the motions is not good enough. Words alone, no matter how religious, have no intrinsic power. On such occasions, prayer is a clash of rival authorities, and the enemy will only yield to the authority that is personally related to Jesus Christ* (*Born for Battle* 96).

So, once again, we must turn to God. We pray. We seek His help, His wisdom, His direction, and His counsel. *We take seriously the fact that Jesus is with us in the battle, that He is fully interested and engaged in the process of winning it on our behalf, and that we will not be left comfortless and without protection from the awful forces that come against us.* God, in His faithfulness, has provided the necessary armor, weapons, and battle plan so that we are protected and equipped for the battle. Ephesians 6 has them listed for us. We do well to spend time studying these provisions for the battle.

We must not miss the importance of prayer in the battle, for it is key to our employing the other provisions God has made for us. I love these old words by William Cowper:

> *What various hindrances we meet*
> *in coming to the mercy seat?*
> *Yet who that knows the worth of prayer,*

Just Before Dawn

> *but wishes to be often there.*
>
> *Prayer makes the darkened cloud withdraw,*
> *prayer climbs the ladder Jacob saw;*
> *gives exercise to faith and love,*
> *brings every blessing from above.*
>
> *Restraining prayer, we cease to fight;*
> *prayer makes the Christian's armor bright;*
> *and Satan trembles, when he sees*
> *the weakest saint upon his knees...*
> *(William Cowper 1779)*

We must do all that we can in order to give ourselves every edge in the battle so that we may enjoy the victory that God intends for us to walk in. II Cor. 2:11 makes it clear that we must not allow the enemy any benefit by our neglect to familiarize ourselves with the methods he will seek to employ in order to discourage and hinder us. *"Lest Satan should get an advantage of us, for we are not ignorant of his devices."*

What kinds of things give the enemy an advantage? Division, hatred, fear, bitterness, resentment, unforgiveness, disobedience, isolation (to name a few). When we remain in a state of willing ignorance and a refusal to become informed we make it easier for the enemy to continue to use his cruel tactics against us. If we are ignorant of the enemy's devices, he certainly will have an advantage over us! Never mistake, dear children of God, the enemy's absolute refusal to allow us to do the work that God has called us to do in peace and security and confidence - at least, not for very long. While the enemy is not creative, he certainly is persistent, and does not willingly give up or give in to the purposes of God for His people easily. The more at stake for the purposes of God, the harder he resists. His hatred for those that God loves most - His people - is intense, and drives him on to seek to thwart them and their work for God in any way that he can.

The Battle

<u>Through Manifold Trials</u>

"Blessed be the God and Father of our Lord Jesus Christ... which hath begotten us unto a lively hope. Wherein ye greatly rejoice, though now for a season, if need be, ye are in heaviness through manifold temptations, that the trial of your faith, being much more precious than of gold that perisheth, though it be tried with fire, might be found unto praise and honor and glory at the appearing of Jesus Christ" (I Pet. 1:3, 6).

So many times we are surprised and dismayed (though we shouldn't be) at the intensity of the conflict going on in and around people's lives these days! Everywhere we turn, it seems, we (or those near us) are dealing with seemingly overwhelming difficulties. These things cause us to want to report to one another at times, as the spies did to the people in Num. 13, *"There are giants in the land, and they are surely too strong for us!"*

We have a choice to make at this point - will we fall into discouragement and choose for ourselves a new captain to lead us back to Egypt or will we quiet ourselves before our great God and declare like a Caleb, *"Let us go up at once and possess the land, for we are well able to overcome it!"* or like Joshua, *"If the Lord delights in us, then He will bring us into this land, and give it us. Neither fear the people of the land...the Lord is with us!"* (Num. 13:30 Num. 14:8 and 9).

It very much depends upon our perspective of Who God is and what that means to us personally, and also our response to the trial and conflict when it comes, as it surely will if we are doing anything at all to affect and further the kingdom of God. Reading again the account of Shadrach, Meshach and Abednego, as they were being questioned by Nebuchadnezzar and before being placed in the fiery furnace of Babylon. Remember what got them in their predicament in the first place? It was their good reputation as servants of the Most

Just Before Dawn

High God*!* *"They regard not thee, O king, nor serve thy gods..." (Dan. 3:12)* The enemies of God are always quick to accuse God's people to "the powers that be" hoping for their hurt, seeking their destruction (Job 1:1, 7-11 Neh. 2:10, 19 4:1, 7, 8 Ezra 4:1,-5 Dan. 3:8, 12 6:3-5, 11-13, etc.!) and he will always be grieved at those who seek the welfare of God's people (Neh. 2:10). It is just such times as these, however, that opportunities arise before us to do what we are ultimately seeking to do anyway - make Him known, prove His worth, and tell of His glory. Nebuchadnezzar himself asked the key question, *"Who is that God that shall deliver you...,"* and this is the very opportunity for God to reveal Himself in a way that perhaps wouldn't come by any other means than the dangerous trial before them.

"Who is that God...?" A good question. What *do* we believe about Him and how will that affect our lives, actions, choices, prayers? God wants to reveal Himself to us, and to make His power and glories known to the world, and He always chooses the best and most effective way of doing that. These men in Daniel 3 knew something about God that circumstances could not affect and outcomes would not change. We need, as servants also of the Most High God, to determine to remain determined even through the most difficult of the trials and conflicts of life that affect and come into our lives. Let us remain determined to keep strong and uncompromising, though all the forces of the enemy be hurled against us and seek to cause us to waver in fear and discouragement. Let us be more "instant in prayer" than ever before, not waiting or wavering or doubting - for this is where we sound forth our battle cry most effectively!

Lastly, remember and be assured, dear warriors of God, that in the end it will be the enemies of God themselves who will be forced to declare His glory and tell of His exploits. "Blessed be the God of Shadrach, Meshach, and Abednego, Who hath sent His angel, and delivered His servants that trusted in Him, and have changed the king's word, and yielded their bodies,

The Battle

that they might not serve nor worship any god, except their own God...*because there is no other God that can deliver after this sort"* (Dan. 3:28 and 29).

As for us, for now, this is our privilege and we will not be robbed of it. "Our God, Whom we serve, is able to deliver us from the burning fiery furnace, and He will deliver us out of your hand, O king. *But if not,* be it known unto thee, O king, that we will not serve thy gods, nor worship the golden image which thou hast set up" (Dan. 3:18).

Yes, we are in "manifold trials and temptations" here, as I Peter 4:10 reminds us, but His grace is manifold, too. God bless each of you as you faithfully press on.

Because of Him,
Karenjoy

So many of us have found that the greatest and most intense and cruel attacks come not from without, but from within. We can be extremely hard on ourselves at times, can't we? As we have said over and again, the battle is for our minds, for our belief system, all coming against our internal rest and assurance that we all long to have in Christ in the innermost parts of our being. It's there that the enemy seeks most to rush in and deal a deathblow to us. It's an insidious, dirty game that he plays with determination, and he plays it as one well practiced in it (for so he is). It is on that front - the battleground for our minds and hearts - that the hardest battles are fought. And there they must be won.

What do I believe about God? Like His disciples long ago, He asks us this question: *"Whom do you say that I am?"* When life is going smoothly, when we can figure out all the reasons, it's not so hard to answer that question, but when sickness strikes, or someone rejects us or treats us unfairly, when we become overwhelmed by the seemingly endless flashbacks and nightmares and triggers that remind us of the horrors of our past, what then? Who can reason or explain abuse??

Just Before Dawn

How could such evil things happen? Why? When we cannot find the answers, *then Whom do we say that Jesus is??* The answer is the same as it was before tragedy happens, or depression strikes, or memories return, or people abandon us. Life may have drastically changed, but God has not *(Mal. 3:6, Heb. 13:8).*

Here is another of those places we exercise our freedom to choose. We can believe whatever we will - about God, about people, about myself, anything or anyone else. God still will not change. He will not run after us, chide us, scold us, shame us, nor beg us to reconsider. He will not force Himself, His will, His perspective, His word, His opinion on us in any way, not even for our own good. *And He will not leave us, either. He will not become angry and walk away.* He will not punish us with distance or silence. He will not go away and abandon us, nor will He hold a grudge against us and treat us differently. *God is not like our abusers.* He is not like those who hurt us. He will patiently, lovingly, willingly wait. *"The Lord waits to be gracious unto thee..." (Isa. 30:18).* His character will not change, ever, nor will His love fail.

> *When crushing sorrow press upon me,*
> *Overwhelm my soul,*
> *When I can no longer look up,*
> *Can no longer hope*
> *Which way can I turn for solace?*
> *Upon whom can I call?*
> *Looking round and round about me*
> *I stumble and I fall...*
>
>
> *Again in desperation*
> *I call upon His Name,*
> *One more time He stoops and lifts me,*
> *Over and again!*

The Battle

> *How many times I've been here, Lord,*
> *In my weakness come,*
> *Come with all my fears and sadness,*
> *Searching for some one...*
> *Jesus! Lord! I'm pleading, Savior!*
> *Listen to my cry!*
> *Over and again I call You,*
> *And must not be denied!*
>
> *So over and again I'll seek*
> *Until I finally find,*
> *Over and again I'll fight*
> *Until I've peace of mind,*
> *For over and again You promised*
> *To heed my heartfelt cry,*
> *So over and again I'll call You,*
> *I will not be denied!*
>
> *Once again in desperation*
> *I'll call upon Your Name,*
> *Once again You'll stoop and lift me,*
> *Faithful once again,*
> *Over and again!*

The battle can take place on other fields, as well, often those we are unfamiliar with, and sadly, unprepared for. The area of Satanic Ritual Abuse is one such battlefield, and it can present some unique challenges, especially in the context of our walk and relationship with God. For those who have been abused in this way, the confusion about the true character and Person of God is extremely difficult to work through. It is in this area that the battle can become most intense. The article below explains:

Trigger Warning For those who have a background of this kind of abuse, please take care of yourself.

Just Before Dawn

Ritual Abuse

For those who have suffered the horrors of Satanic Ritual Abuse, the lies become even more convoluted because there is such a blatant anti-God message that is an intrinsic part of the abuse. We are taught that we are *personally* responsible (and to blame!) for what happened on the cross, and that we are beyond the provisions God has made for the redemption of His people.

We are "programmed" and led to believe that the demonic realm is much more powerful than it really is - and to a child who is forced to witness the horridness of what takes place at rituals there is more than enough "proof" to see to it that those beliefs are deeply implanted!

The scriptures are twisted and used as weapons to "prove" our guilt and unpardonable sinfulness, instead of bringing the hope and comfort that others reading the same verses might receive. We have been forced to "pray" and "confess" these things in the most humiliating circumstances, and the fear of that recurring is unimaginably (to those who haven't experienced this) terrifying.

Cults are especially adept at setting their victims up in double bind (no win, darned-if-you-do-and-darned-if-you-don't) situations. It is the ultimate "proof" of our powerlessness and leaves us hopeless of *ever* finding a way out.

Satanism is all about defiling what is holy and most precious to God, and because the enemy is the master of deception, he does everything that he can to turn us away from God by instilling his deeply entrenched lies about Him within our very beings. It is the cruelest and most insidious form of the abuse of a child. BUT there really is good news in spite of the enemy's malicious whisperings; to the contrary, *God is the Redeemer!* ***Despite what lies our abusers taught us about Him or how they blamed and accused Him, His grace really is sufficient for us; His provision really is complete, His promises really do apply, and His arm really is that long and strong.*** He is more than able to reach us even down the deepest depths of

The Battle

hopelessness and despair. There is absolutely nothing too hard for Him!

The Problem With Christian Symbols in SRA

Symbols are significant because of the meaning behind them, the importance we attach to them. For those whose abuse was spiritual in nature, as in Satanic Ritual Abuse (SRA), the thought of regeneration (or anything having to do with Christianity and church attendance) may not sound appealing at all. Satan has gone out of his way to try to distort every religious symbol he can in order to make those things that should represent life and hope to become something that brings up images of death and defeat. Symbols change meaning when the stories they represent have been altered, and because of this, SRA survivors will see these symbols differently than those whose perspectives are derived from the true Biblical narratives and intentions of God behind them.

From a Christian perspective, for example, symbols such as the cross remind us of redemption, salvation, and new life, but to a Ritual Abuse survivor, the cross represents nothing of the sort! Instead of a willing and triumphant sacrifice of love and forgiveness it reminds us of the horror and suffering we witnessed at rituals.

Blood is another very difficult Biblical symbol. To the Christian, "the blood of Christ," and what it represents is a conceptual symbol, but it is quite literal to one who has seen blood used in rituals. The images of the blood of Jesus bringing cleansing from sin and new life to the believer are the opposite of the defilement and death that it reminds an SRA survivor of. Being "covered with the blood" is not something we can hear without horrible images of being literally covered with the blood of those sacrifices we observed at rituals coming to mind.

What about the elements of the Lord's Table, the bread and the wine? Partaking of Communion is one of the most difficult Christian observances for survivors of SRA. Because this symbol has been one of the most cruelly distorted of all (as in the Black Mass) it can cause some of the most painful memories and flashbacks to surface.

Phrases such as "Bride of Christ," which should bring joy and glad expectation, are cruel reminders of the bondage we have been drawn into by being "wedded" to Satan, a common ritual theme.

We could go on and on, because the incredible number of distorted symbols abound, but rather than doing that, we want to make the point that certain symbols, and the meanings we attach to them, are intrinsically tied to the experiences behind them. What we came to believe as a result of the 'lessons' learned (through horrific experience) will also result in distortions in our beliefs. Because the biblical teachings have been distorted and made to mean things they never should have, they must be retold from a new perspective, again and again.

How many times does it take to change the distorted story surrounding the "good" symbol to correct it? The only answer may be, until the things they remind us of have been redeemed by God Himself in our lives.

Who hears the silent scream?
or comforts her despair?
Who halts the plundering?
or seeks for her repair?
A city, broken without cause,
whose walls have been brought down,
in ruins, defenseless, without hope.
no living voices sound -
only specters, wandering, remain
bemoaning all their loss,
seeking rest but finding none.
Her sorrow flows like dross
thrown upon the scrap pile heap
the craftsmen toss away.
Is there no help or recompense?
No halting the decay?

The Battle

> *It was upon the scrap pile heap*
> *He found her passing by.*
> *He looked upon her brokenness,*
> *and He began to cry.*
> *He stooped and gathered all her parts*
> *and took them in His arms,*
> *and shielding them from further hurt*
> *He kept them safe and warm.*
> *And nurturing and loving her*
> *He brought her back to health.*
> *He took her from her low estate*
> *and brought her into wealth.*
> *Not silver, gold, or earthly stores*
> *did He entrap her with,*
> *but that unfading, lasting kind*
> *earth's richest do possess.*
> *No substitute, but heaven's best*
> *He with her did endow,*
> *and set a crown of Kingly love*
> *upon her wondering brow.*

Is anything too hard for God? Is healing, even from the horrors of the most unspeakable forms of abuse, beyond His ability to accomplish? The answer is, undeniably, *no*. No matter how loudly the enemy threatens or resists or seeks to hinder us in the battle, we will not surrender. No matter how persistently he seeks to thwart us by his attempts us to convince us that we are powerless and without hope, we will not yield. Remember Nehemiah 4. No matter how brazenly he asserts that daylight will never shine upon us again, we will not give way to despair. The fact remains that *He Who is in us is greater*, and that truth is not up for deliberation.

> *"Nevertheless we made our prayer unto our God, and set a watch against them day and night..."* Nehemiah 4:9

Just Before Dawn

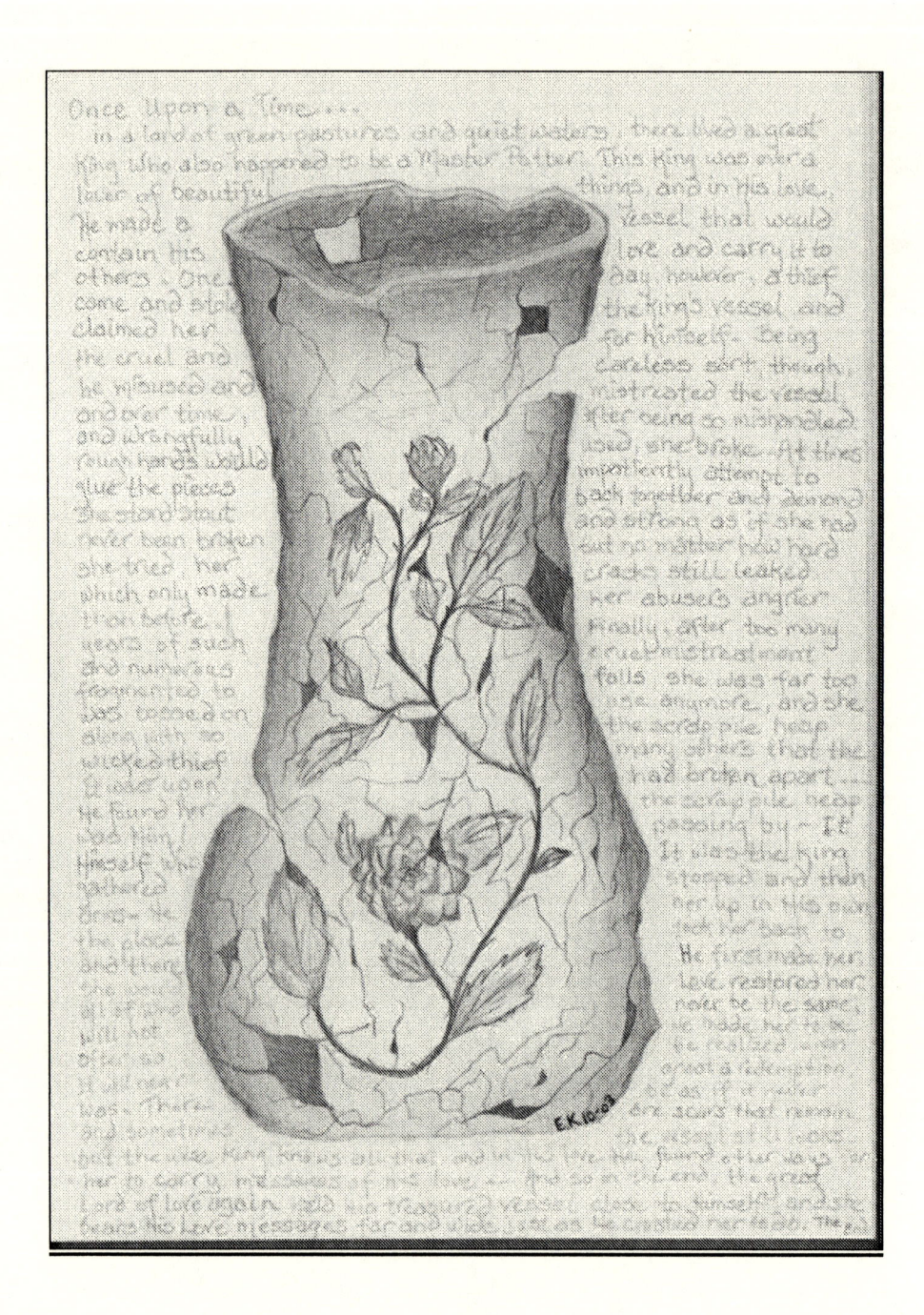

The Battle

Once upon a time

Once upon a time, in a land of green pastures and quiet waters, there lived a great King Who also happened to be a Master Potter. This King was ever a lover of beautiful things, and in His love, He made a vessel that would contain His love and carry it to others.

One day, however, a thief came and stole the King's vessel and claimed her for himself. Being the cruel and careless sort, though, he misused and mistreated the vessel, and over time, after being so mishandled and wrongfully used, she broke. At times rough hands would impatiently attempt to pick her up and glue the pieces back together, and then demand that she stand stout and strong, as if she had never been broken at all, but no matter how hard she tried, her cracks still leaked, which only made her abusers angrier than before. Finally, after too many years of such cruel mistreatment and numerous falls, she was far too fragmented to use anymore, and she was tossed on the scrap pile heap along with so many others that the wicked thief had broken apart.

It was there upon that scrap heap that the King found her one day as He was passing by. It was Him! It was her King! He saw her there, and quickly stooped and gathered her up in His own arms. He took her back to the place he first made her and the work of repair began. Love restored here there.

She will never be the same again; of course, it will never be as if it never was. Scars remain, and sometimes the vessel still leaks, but the wise King knows all that, and in His love He found other ways for her to carry messages of His love. And so in the end, the great Lord of Love again held His treasured vessel close to Himself, redeemed and restored, and she does bear His Love messages far and wide, just as He and she had always longed for her to do.

Afterwards

When comes the dawn at last
The long black nighttime finally past
I will arise and sing and tell
My Lord and God did all things well!

Is healing really possible? Is it really worth all of the pain, all of the sacrifice and the terrible cost? I can't count how many times I've been asked that question over the years. That's okay; I asked it, too.

Looking back from where I am now, I can see that the journey was indeed a long and difficult one, but it was worth it, because it brought me to my present vantage point. I can see now, and I love the view.
I know that unless I'd gone through "there" I would never have arrived "here."

I've learned so much along the way - about God, about people, about myself and my relationship to it all. I am convinced in a way that I never was before that I have indeed been fearfully and wonderfully made. We each have. And I know that despite what my abusers told me, God is good, His Word is true, and He is not responsible for my pain and abuse.

Life as I am able to live it now is a marvel for me. The "abundant life" truly does exist. His joy does indeed give strength. The promises of God are true. He has done above and beyond all that I ever could have imagined or hoped or thought, and I have had, and do have, the present-day privilege of not only watching and seeing the hand of God at work in and through my own life and that of others, but I am also actually a front-line participant in the healing process. Imagine! He invited me, and because He also gave me the courage to respond, I am here.

I remember reading a quote by Ernest Hemingway once that touched me so deeply. It said, *"The world breaks everyone, and afterward, some are strong at the broken places."* I wanted it to be like that for me, wanted God to do that kind of marvelous thing in me. How faithful He has been. I stand in awe.

At a time in my life when my level of hope was lowest, God promised me something in Ezekiel 36, and then He came through, just as He said that He could and would. He said that that all the waste places and all the desolate places inside me would be filled with life. They are. He said that my bleak internal landscape would be tilled and that it would become like the garden of Eden. It is. He said that the waste and desolated and ruined places inside me would be fortified and inhabited, and that new life would be restored within me. It has. Then He said that those round about me would know that He, the Lord, had rebuilt the ruined places, and replanted that which had been destroyed. They do. He said He would do all those things and more, and He has. It was the promises of God (and my desperate hope in them) that got me through the process, and I am a walking, talking, living and breathing testimony that He is Who He says He is, and that nothing is too hard for Him. Though I feared it, I was not too far away or beyond His reach, I was not beyond His willingness or ability to redeem and restore, and His love and mercy and grace really could extend to the likes of "even me." They have. And I am glad beyond words and expression. Thank You, O Most High God.

My earnest prayer is that those who have experienced the brokenness and devastation that results from man's cooperation with the enemy of our souls, and his cruel intent against them, would be able to walk in hope once again, the pure Hope that God meant for each of His children to walk in and enjoy. Truth sets free, no matter what enslaves us. May the truths shared in this book bring light into the darkness and nighttime of the devastating aftermath of abuse. May we indeed look up toward the face of the Living God and know that Day Light is coming. Hold on, dear child of God, joy comes in the morning! This dark hour is indeed the one just before dawn.

Because of Him,
Pam

Afterwards

> *"Yet the Lord shall command His loving kindness in the daytime, and in the night His song shall be with me, and my prayer to the God of my life" (Ps. 42:8).*

> *"For Thou wilt light my candle, the Lord my God will enlighten my darkness" (Ps. 18:28).*

Resources

Born For Battle R. Arthur Matthews (1978)
    Harold Shaw Publishers; Wheaton, IL

Boundaries Henry Cloud, PhD & John Townsend, PhD (1992)
    Zondervan Publishing House; Grand Rapids, MI

Diagnostic and Statistical Manual of Mental Disorders, Fourth Edition, Text Revision (2000)
    American Psychiatric Association; Washington, DC

False Assumptions: Twelve "Christian" Beliefs That Can Drive You Crazy Henry Cloud, PhD & John Townsend, PhD (1994)
    Zondervan Publishing House; Grand Rapids, MI

Healing the Shame That Binds You John Bradshaw (1988)
    Health Communications, Inc; Deerfield Beach, FL

Living From the Heart Jesus Gave You James G. Friesen, Ph.D (et al) (2000) Shepherd's house, Inc; Pasadena, CA

Safe People Henry Cloud, Ph.D & John Townsend, Ph.D (1995)
    Zondervan Publishing House; Grand Rapids, MI

The Search for Significance Robert S. McGee (1990).
    Rapha Publishing; Houston, TX

Trauma and Recovery Judith Herman, M.D. (1992)
    Basic Books; New York, NY

Unchained Memories Lenore Terr, M.D. (1994)
    Basic Books; New York, NY

Uncovering The Mystery of MPD James Friesen, Ph.D (1991)
    Here's Life Publishers; San Bernardino, CA

Resources

Verbal Abuse Survivors Speak Out Patricia Evans (1993)
   Bob Adams, Inc.; Holbrook, MA

The Wounded Heart Dan Allender, Ph.D (1990)
   NavPress; Colorado Springs, CO

Suggested Reading

Beyond the Darkness Cynthia Kubetin & James Mallory, M.D. (1992) Rapha Publishing/Word, Inc.; Houston & Dallas, TX

Breaking the Circle of Satanic Ritual Abuse Daniel Ryder (1992) CompCare Publishers; Minneapolis, MN

The Bondage Breaker Neil T. Anderson (1990) Harvest House Publishers; Eugene, OR

The Faces of Rage: Resolving the Losses That Lead to Anger, Guilt, Shame David Damico (1992) NavPress; Colorado Springs, CO

Faith That Hurts Faith That Heals: Understanding the Fine Line Between Healthy Faith & Spiritual Abuse Stephen Arterburn & Jack Felton (1992) Thomas Nelson Publishers; Nashville, TN

Grace Grows Best In Winter Margaret Clarkson (1972) Zondervan Corporation; Grand Rapids, MI

The Healing Path Dan Allender (1999) WaterBrook Press; Colorado Springs, CO

Healing the Hardware of the Soul Daniel Amen, M.D. (2002) Free Press; New York, NY

Inside Out Dr. Larry Crabb (1988) NavPress Publishing Group; Colorado Springs, CO

Many Minds: Information for People Who Have Multiple Personality Disorder Lauren Lund & David Lund (1993) Soft Words Publishing; Pueblo, CO

Suggested Reading

Multiple Personality Disorder From the Inside Out (1991)
   Sidran Press; Baltimore, MD

On the Threshold of Hope Diane Mandt Langberg, Ph.D (1999)
   Tyndale House Publishers; Wheaton, IL

Ritual Abuse: What It Is, Why It Happens, and What To Do About It
   Margaret Smith (1993)
   Harper Collins Publishing; New York, NY

The Scarred Soul: Understanding and Ending Self-Inflicted Violence
   Tracy Alderman (1997)
   New Harbinger Publications, Inc.; Oakland, CA

Seeing Behind the Masks Jim Toombs (1995)
   Questar Publishing; Sisters, OR

Spiritual Warfare for the Wounded Dr. Mark Johnson (1992)
   Servant Publications; Ann Arbor, MI 48107

Taking Every Thought Captive Alaine Pakkala (1995)
   Lydia Press; Colorado Springs, CO

Victims No Longer: Men Recovering From Incest and Other Sexual Abuse Mike Lew (1988)
   Harper & Row Publishers; New York, NY

Just Before Dawn

Counselor Resources

The Biblical Basis of Christian Bounseling for People Helpers
  Gary R. Collins, Ph.D (2001)
  NavPress Publishing Group; Colorado Springs, CO

The Body Remembers: The Psychophysiology of Trauma and Trauma Treatment Rothschild, Babette (2000)
  W.W. Norton & Company, Inc.; New York, London

Counseling Survivors of Sexual Abuse Diane Langberg, Ph.D (1997)
  Tyndale House Publishers; Wheaton, IL

Managing Traumatic Stress Through Art: Drawing From the Center
  Barry M. Cohen, Mary-Michola Barnes &Anita B. Rankin (1995) The Sidran Press; Lutherville, MD

Psychological Trauma Bessel A. van der Kolk, M.D. (1987)
  American Psychiatric Press, Inc.; Wahington, DC

Trauma and Survival Elizabeth Waites (1993)
  W.W. Norton & Company, Inc.; New York, London

Trauma and Recovery: The Aftermath of Violence-From Domestic Abuse to Political Terror Judith Herman, M.D. (1997)
  BasicBooks; New York, NY

The Way of the Journal: A Journal Therapy Workbook for Healing
  Kathleen Adams, MA, LPC (1998)
  The Sidran Press; Lutherville, MD

Counselor Resources

Index

Abuse, 80, 95, 155, 191, 214, 215, 225, 226, 236, 238, 239
Addictions, 189
Ambivalence, 33
Anorexia, 189, 196
Anxiety, 76, 78, 88, 138, 167
Body memories, 2, 10, 20, 53, 57, 94, 96, 137, 138, 147, 159, 168, 223, 227
Bonds, 29, 188, 202
Bulimia, 189, 196
Coping Mechanisms, 137, 166
Depression, 169, 170, 180
Despair, 82
DID (Dissociative Identity Disorder), 137, 138, 139, 140, 166
Dissociation, 137, 138, 139, 165
Fear, 88, 89, 90
Fibromyalgia, 180
Flashbacks, 20, 50, 147, 166, 168, 196, 222, 227
Forgiveness, 97, 100, 104, 107, 158

Hope, 21, 38, 39, 84, 101, 119, 120, 123, 140, 141, 142, 148, 149, 151, 152, 160, 171, 233, 238
Insomnia, 196
Joy, 184
MPD (Multiple Personality Disorder), 137, 166, 235
Multiple Personality Disorder, 137, 139, 238
Neediness, 65
Panic attack, 77, 213
Post Traumatic Stress Disorder, 140, 166, 167, 169
PTSD, 166, 167, 168
Satanic Ritual Abuse, 145, 224, 225, 226, 237
Self-injury, 189
Shame, 31, 32, 33, 35, 98, 235, 237
Spiritual Abuse, 237
SRA (Satanic Ritual Abuse), 147, 226
Stress, 169, 180, 239
Suicidal thoughts, 171
Trust, 36, 37, 56, 86

Index

Just Before Dawn

We would appreciate your feedback!

Please send questions and comments to:

Pamela Perez
Just Before Dawn
P.O. Box 1604
Yucaipa, CA 92399

Or e-mail me at jb4dawn@lycos.com

Thank you!

Index

About the Author

In her work as a Biblical lay counselor, Pam specializes in ministering to survivors of severe abuse. From individual counseling to leading small groups, she uses her knowledge and experience regarding healing from abuse to equip survivors for the process, with its pitfalls and triumphs. Additionally, Pam is an inspirational conference and retreat speaker who possesses a rare insight into the complex and difficult issues surrounding the spiritual aspects of healing from abuse.

Printed in the United States
16029LVS00006B/214-267